# *Test Pilot*

Neville Duke

The name of Neville Duke is well-known in aviation circles, not only as a successful wartime fighter pilot, but also as a peacetime test pilot with the Hawker Aviation Company.

Joining the RAF at the beginning of the war, he found himself as a young fighter pilot with the crack 92 Squadron at RAF Biggin Hill, in 1941. That spring and summer he survived the air battles over Northern France with the Biggin Hill Wing, often flying as wingman to the legendary 'Sailor' Malan—Fighter Command's top-scoring pilot at that time. In those months he learnt the fighter pilot's trade, lessons that were to prove invaluable when, in November, he was posted to a very different air war in the Western Desert.

Flying the famous 'Shark Mouthed' P40E Tomahawk fighters, he quickly established himself as one of the most successful pilots in North Africa, winning the DFC and bar. By 1943 he was flight commander with his old 92 Squadron, which had also become part of the Desert Air Force.

Again flying Spitfires, he brought his score to twenty-one by the end of the Tunisian Campaign, was awarded the DSO, then given command of 145 Spitfire Squadron in Italy. Leading this unit in the summer of 1944 he brought his score to twenty-eight, receiving a second bar to his DFC.

Towards the end of the war he became an RAF test pilot and later a member of the RAF's High Speed Flight. This was the start of a successful career as a test pilot after leaving the Service in 1948, having been awarded the AFC. Working for Hawkers, he became Chief Test Pilot and did all the major flight development on one of the most famous of all RAF peacetime aircraft—the Hawker Hunter, and with it took the world speed record in 1953.

Injured in a Hunter crash two years later, he was forced to leave Hawkers but continued to fly and later set up his own test flying business, as well as becoming the personal pilot of Sir George Dowty. He worked for years as a freelance and highly respected test pilot, flying the Optica, Fieldmaster and Firemaster aeroplanes. He still flies his own plane.

# Test Pilot

*by Neville Duke*

*in collaboration with*
*Alan W Mitchell*

GRUB STREET · LONDON

First published in 1953

This edition first published in hardback in 1992 by
Grub Street
The Basement
10 Chivalry Road
London SW11 1HT

Reprinted in paperback in 1997

Copyright this edition © 2003 Grub Street, London
Text © Neville Duke

Reprinted 2004

A catalogue record of this book is available from the British Library

Typeset by Rowan Typesetters, Birchington, Kent
Printed and bound in Great Britain by
Biddles Ltd, King's Lynn, Norfolk

With thanks to Norman Franks

TEST PILOT was first published in 1953. This new edition is reprinted
exactly as that edition but with an additional chapter covering Neville
Duke's flying life from that date, and also has appendices and index,
not included in the earlier book, together with a completely new selection
of photographs.

Cover photos show Neville Duke on the day he set the 100km closed
circuit record, 19 September 1953. The front cover image is supplied
courtesy of Brian Isles, and with thanks to him.

Cover design by Hugh Adams at AB3

*To all my Fellow Pilots*
*of the War years*
*and today.*

# *Contents*

# List of Illustrations

# *Introduction*

DURING the clear, sunny afternoon of 6th September, 1952 many thousands of spectators at the annual display of the Society of British Aircraft Constructors peered into the sky above Farnborough aerodrome, their eyes seeking the DH 110, a twin-tailed fighter aircraft with swept wings, flown by John Derry, test pilot of the De Havilland Aircraft Company. With Anthony Richards as his observer, Derry dived from a height of over 40,000 feet towards Farnborough, causing sonic explosions like rumbling gunfire. As the echoes died, the DH 110 swept low over the aerodrome to begin an aerobatic display.

Suddenly, the crowd's admiration changed to horror. Without warning the aircraft broke up, littering the sky with drifting wreckage; its cockpit fell on to the runway, and its two engines hurtled through the air like shells into a section of the spectators.

In that tense atmosphere, while the injured and the dead were yet uncounted and the ruin of the DH 110 was still being cleared from the runway, Neville Duke, chief test pilot of the Hawker Aircraft Company, took off in the sleek, graceful Hawker Hunter. He was watched in silence, all eyes seeking his return. He dived, causing sonic explosions, and reproduced the perfect exhibition of flying he had given during the earlier days of the display.

Men and women, while biting on the thought that his aircraft, too, might break up, felt their hearts lift to his cool nerve and example, wondering in their minds what his thoughts might be at that moment.

The news of the accident, and of Neville Duke's immediate flight, went out to the world, and sorrow was mingled with admiration. Among the millions who read and heard the news, one sat down to pen a note— the Prime Minister, Sir Winston Churchill. We have Sir Winston's permission to quote it. "My dear Duke," he wrote, "It was characteristic

10

of you, and of 615 Squadron, to go up yesterday after the shocking accident. Accept my salute."

The next day while the accident and its possible causes were still being widely discussed, Neville Duke again took up the Hunter, producing sonic explosions in cloud, and performing aerobatics over the spot where Derry and Richards had crashed. He flew brilliantly.

These incidents, and general interest in supersonic flying by test pilots, concentrated attention on Neville Duke. This book, a story of his career and experiences, is a result of that attention.

There are one or two things I should like to say. Neville had to be persuaded to tell his story; he did so reluctantly. If there should be a suspicion that he "line shoots" then I alone am to blame. But if you should find interest and pleasure in this book, then the credit must go to Neville Duke. For it is his story. His experiences during the last war are drawn from his own war diaries, several passages being quoted verbatim.

Flying, the thrill and joy of it, have been and are his life. He regards success and renown as being incidental. For him aircraft are machines that come to life while he flies them; and he flies with enthusiasm, part boyish, part the mature aviator. He is a superlative pilot who looks always ahead to the future, and he works hard and seriously.

When his test flying days are ended let us expect there will be found for him a niche in aviation where the deep well of his experience and knowledge may be drawn upon for many years to come.

Alan W Mitchell

*Westhumble,*
*Dorking, Surrey.*

# CHAPTER 1

## *Through the Hatch!*

I DISCOVERED that I had flown faster than sound for the first time when I went into my office in the control tower of Hawker's airfield at Dunsfold one morning.

It is a comfortable office, with cream walls, a fawn carpet, a roomy desk and chair, and with photographs of aircraft here and there. An adjoining office is used by four more of Hawker's test pilots—Frank Murphy, Frank Bullen, Bill Bedford, and Donald Lucey.

I popped my head through a hatch-way in the wall. Frank Bullen was sitting at his desk, puffing away contentedly at his pipe.

"Morning, Frank," I said.

He removed his pipe, gave me a large smile, and replied, "Morning, Nev. Quite a good one yesterday, eh?"

"What?" I asked, puzzled.

We looked at one another for a moment or two, as though we were in the middle of a guessing game.

Then Frank said, "Yes, you nearly made my wife jump out of her skin."

The penny dropped.

"What?" I repeated. "A bang?"

"Yes, a beauty," Frank answered. "Didn't you know?"

Frank left his chair and came over to the hatch. He lives about twelve miles away from Dunsfold in North Chapel, a village near Ball's Cross, which is not far away from Petworth, in Sussex. When he had driven through Ball's Cross on his way home the previous evening he had seen a small knot of villagers talking together, and pulled up his car.

"Anything wrong at Hawker's today, Mr. Bullen?" he was asked. "Wasn't a crash, was there?"

Frank said no there had been no crash, and that nothing was wrong.

12

One elderly man, with a flowing white beard, remarked, "Then it must have been one of they queer bangs".

One of they queer bangs! Frank guessed what it was, a supersonic explosion. He knew I had been flying that day, and supposed that I knew that I had caused a bang.

I had been up with the Hawker Hunter and had dived from the area just above the Hog's Back in the direction of Chichester. I knew that I must have been moving at somewhere near the speed of sound, for the needle on the Machmeter had worked up to a little over 1; but you always have to take minor errors into account and you can never be quite sure of your exact speed.

There was no doubt that I must have passed over Ball's Cross, or somewhere near it. And there could be no doubt now that I had flown faster than sound, or had passed through what they call the sound barrier.

I felt quite pleased about it; and I think that Sir Sydney Camm, the chief designer at Hawker's, and everybody else there were pretty pleased about it, too. We had all been working for some time to fly the Hunter faster than sound; and although we did not celebrate that particular flight, Frank's news was certainly good.

It probably sounds a pretty dull way of finding out that I had reached supersonic speed for the first time—a chat through a hatch in the office wall.

But you don't really say, "Right! We'll take it up tomorrow afternoon at three and see whether the thing will go through the sound barrier."

There is a lot of long, grinding work for everyone; and it is a team effort, with the test pilot finishing off the job. To explain how it was that I did not know I had flown faster than sound until I had that talk with Frank Bullen, let me run through briefly what happened.

The Hawker Hunter was designed by Sir Sydney Camm and his team, to meet an Air Ministry specification for a new fighter. This did not stipulate in so many words that the new aircraft would have to achieve a transonic speed, but it was fairly obvious that we should have to produce something that would exceed the speed of sound if the specification were to be met.

Work on the designs and construction began in 1948, and the new fighter was known as P—for prototype—1067. It was built at Hawker's factory at Kingston, and it was three years before I eventually took it up for the first test flight, in July 1951.

It flew smoothly from the start. Actually, you do not take a prototype out to the end of a runway and go off in it straight away on a first flight. First, you do taxiing tests along the runway, checking brakes and ground handling; and eventually work up towards take-off speed. When you are happy about all this, then you lift the aircraft up into the air for a couple of hundred yards or so, trying to assess elevator, rudder, and aileron "feel", and establishing the correct trim setting for take-off. Finally, when everything is working to your satisfaction, up you go on your first flight.

All aircraft seem to have their own character and personality—very much like horses. You can tell almost immediately, whether they are going to be "friendly" or "unfriendly". I made friends with the Hunter immediately and I seemed to feel at home in it at once.

There was quite a lot of work to do before I could take it up to over 40,000 feet to begin testing it for supersonic flight. There were the usual tests that have to come first for any new aircraft. These include the clearing of minor snags or faults; general handling tests, measurement of the rate of climb, times required to reach various heights, level speed tests, stability, manoeuvrability and so on. All this means flying when the weather is right, sometimes two or three times a day.

Each time I came down from a flight in the Hunter, I reported everything to our design team who would decide what modifications should be made, and then I would try out the Hunter again to test the effect of these changes. It was a pretty long job, and it took many hours of flying spread over six months before we could begin working up the Hunter to supersonic flight. But it was all tremendously interesting. There is terrific satisfaction in flying a new aircraft and in doing all the development work; and in being the only man to fly it in its early days.

Before we go up to 40,000 feet and talk about flying at high speed, I will try to explain a few things that may sound rather complicated.

For a start, we do not know all that much about supersonic flight at the moment. The whole subject is in its early days, and you might say that test pilots doing this work are explorers.

But there are various things we do know. For instance, it is common knowledge that the speed of sound varies with height, due to change in air temperature. Air temperature falls with altitude; the higher you go, the colder it gets. In simple terms, the recognized figures for air temperature are plus 15 degrees Centigrade at sea level and minus 56 degrees Centigrade at 36,000 feet. Theoretically the air temperature remains constant above this height. Atmospheric pressure also falls with height.

The speed of sound is higher in warmer air than it is in colder. At sea level in standard temperatures, the speed of sound is 760 miles an hour. At 36,000 feet it falls to 660 miles an hour; and since it depends upon air temperature, it remains the same—or constant at 660 miles an hour—above 36,000 feet.

To show pilots how fast they are flying in relation to the speed of sound, we have a Machmeter. It is very much like a speedometer in a car, except that it shows the decimals of 1; and 1 is the speed of sound.

So, if you are flying just above sea level, and the needle on the Machmeter gets on to the 1 you are flying at just about 760 miles an hour. If you are at 36,000 feet and the needle is on the 1, then you are doing about 660 miles an hour true airspeed.

There is a great difference between true airspeed and indicated airspeed. For instance, while flying at 400 miles an hour at sea level, the true and the indicated airspeeds of an aircraft are roughly the same. But at 20,000 feet, although the aircraft may still be travelling at 400 miles an hour, the speed indicated will be about 100 miles per hour less. This is because the pressure of the air is less at that height, the air being thinner, and less pressure is measured by the air speed indicator. And since air pressure decreases the higher you go, so there is a steady fall in indicated speed as you climb, although your true speed remains the same.

At 36,000 feet, and Mach 1, your true airspeed is 660 miles an hour, while your indicated speed is only about 330 miles an hour. If you are flying at an indicated air speed of 330 miles an hour, the strain on an aircraft structure is much less than if you are flying at an indicated airspeed of 760 miles an hour. This is one reason why tests of an aircraft's Mach number characteristics are carried out at high altitude.

As you begin to work up towards the speed of sound at any height— we call it working up to a high Mach number—various effects may be felt by an aircraft. They are the results of compressibility—the air being pressed harder as an aircraft flies faster and nears sonic velocity.

Compressibility may cause such things as vibration, buffeting and pitching. Sometimes the controls may be affected. We call all these various effects "Mach number characteristics". Every time they develop, something on the aircraft has to be changed so that flight at a higher Mach number becomes normal.

But that is enough about technicalities for the time being. It may help to give you a rough idea about some of the problems of working up towards a very high speed.

Let us get ready to go up to between 40,000 and 45,000 feet to start studying Mach number characteristics; because a high Mach number can be obtained more readily in the rarefied air.

After all the initial testing, you have got the feel of the Hunter; and you are at home in it. You could say it is now rather like riding a horse that you have broken in yourself; you know each other pretty well, and you are about to try out a few gallops.

It is important to feel at home in your aircraft when you are eight or nine miles high, testing out something new and, perhaps, at a high Mach number.

You sit in a pressurized cabin, but anything may happen on a test flight and if the perspex hood should crack or break—well, things would happen quickly.

So you have to wear special equipment, and to breathe pure oxygen all the time. In fact, you do not breathe oxygen so much as have it pumped into your lungs; because the air is so thin at high altitudes that if you were breathing in oxygen normally you could exist for some ten minutes only at 45,000 feet and about ten seconds at 50,000 feet.

Your special equipment is a pressurized waistcoat. It covers the whole of the upper part of your body, except the arms; it is laced at the back, and it has a zip-fastener up the front. The waistcoat is double-skinned, and is connected to the main oxygen system. Oxygen inflates the waistcoat and flows into your face mask. This mask has to be sealed tightly on to your face so that there are no leakages; and oxygen coming out of the bottles at pressure is forced into your lungs.

The result is that your breathing action is reversed. Normally you breathe in, making an effort, and then relax and let the air go out of your lungs. But with this waistcoat and mask you make no effort to breathe, but you do have to make an effort to expel the air from your lungs. It is not altogether comfortable, and it makes talking over the radio rather difficult. The pressurized waistcoat, however, is extremely important and valuable; it increases your safe operating height by about 4,000 feet and, if necessary you can fly up to about 44,000 to 45,000 feet without a pressure cabin.

In addition to radio—your link with the control tower at the airfield—you also have a wire-recorder. With this you can chatter away to yourself while you are flying, knowing that everything you say is recorded. When you land you give the recorder to your secretary, who plays it back, listens to it, and types out everything you have said. It is very useful because you can talk about anything to do with the flight while you think of it: how the aircraft behaves at certain speeds, how you feel physically, weather conditions, the engine pressure and temperature figures, the trimmer angles—in fact anything at all, without having to bother about trying to write on the test pad. This pad, with a stop-watch, is strapped on to your right knee—just for making a few more notes if you feel like it.

As for clothing, you normally wear sufficient for comfort and protection at altitude in case the cockpit heating system should fail or you have to abandon the aircraft.

I usually wear a form of crash helmet, especially designed for protection in rough air at high speed, or for crashlanding; or in case of failure of the canopy covering the cockpit.

So let's climb into the Hunter. You go up a ladder, placed by one of the ground staff; and you are probably surprised at the smallness of the cockpit. You sit in an ejector seat, which has a dinghy-pack in case you have to bale out over the sea; and there is a parachute just at your back. If you do have to bale out, there is a handle which you can pull to jettison the perspex canopy. There is a second handle above and behind your head, and you pull this to operate the ejector seat. It brings a blind down over your face and, at the same time, the action of pulling the handle fires two cartridges which shoot the seat right out of the cockpit. You have to be shot out in this way, because otherwise the pressure of airflow at high speed would keep you inside the aircraft.

As you sit in the Hunter, it is like being in a lowish, comfortable chair, with your legs resting easily on the rudder bars and the control column between your knees. There are a number of instruments to keep an eye on, but the main ones are slightly below your eye level and easy to check. They are the altimeter, to watch the height; the airspeed indicator, to give the indicated airspeed; and the Machmeter, to show how fast you are going in relation to the speed of sound at any altitude. You also keep an eye on the pressurization system and the cabin altimeter, which shows the pressure of the atmosphere in the cockpit compared with the pressure of the atmosphere outside. There are also many other things to watch, like fuel gauges, oil pressure, jet pipe temperature and engine revolutions per minute, hydraulic pressure and so on.

So there you are—pretty well tied up in a neat bundle, sitting in the Hunter ready to start taxiing, the oxygen mask pinching your face, the earphones crackling a bit, the oxygen pumping in cold puffs, and the jet engine sounding rather like a vacuum cleaner going in the next room.

On the left hand side of the cockpit is the throttle. You ease it forward and taxi down to the end of the runway, checking your radio with flying control as you go. At the end of the 2,000 yard runway you put on the brakes, and make a thorough cockpit check for trim, fuel, hood, pressures, temperatures. One point not checked, or overlooked, may mean trouble.

Now you are ready to take off. You move the throttle forward and smoothly open up the engine on the brakes; and, after checking the power, let the brakes off. As the brakes are released and full power applied, the aircraft fairly leaps forward and accelerates. You can feel the pressure on your back as it surges forward. The runway seems to race at you.

Taking off in the Hunter is a great thrill. You get a terrific sense of speed, especially as there seems to be nothing of the nose of the aircraft in front of you on the other side of the bullet-proof glass. While the ground races underneath, suddenly the Hunter seems to come to life. It reacts to your slightest movement—just a touch of the finger tips and it does exactly what you want it to do. It rides smoothly over the long broad blackish runway stretching away ahead of you and looking like a great wide main road. When the speed is right, you gently ease back on the control column, and the ground just melts away.

You climb pretty quickly in the Hunter, more quickly than in any other aircraft I have flown; and it is not long before you are at 30,000 feet and you begin to get a feeling of detachment and remoteness. With me, this always increases with height; until at about 40,000 to 45,000 feet I sometimes get a pleasant feeling of loneliness. The world below seems far away.

It is quite exhilarating flying at this height, too. The sky above you is without a suspicion of cloud. It is a very deep blue, a beautiful colour, sapphire and very clean-looking. If there are clouds below, this deep blue of the sky somehow seems to give them a dead-white appearance so that they look as though they have been thoroughly washed; and they are usually crinkled or seem moulded into definite patterns. The sun is terrifically bright, and if you are staying up at this height for long it is just as well to have tinted goggles. Everything seems very clean and new; and very quiet and smooth. If there is no cloud bank below you can see the earth looking rather greyish and the sea rather black; and it is almost as though you were looking at a big ill-defined map. You have very little sense of speed because there is nothing going past; and sometimes you feel as though you are just suspended there.

But we haven't come up to look at the view! The job is to start testing the Mach number characteristics. This is done by flying straight and level and carefully increasing speed, watching the Mach number getting higher, or rather the Mach needle registering on a higher number, until maybe you begin to notice that the aircraft is not behaving as it should. It may be that it is vibrating slightly, or buffeting or pitching—the nose of the aircraft beginning to go up and down a little. Or it may be that you find that the controls are not answering as they should do. Whatever happens, you talk away to yourself, trying to describe every detail, however small, knowing that all you say is being picked up by the wire recorder. When you feel that you have enough information about the aircraft's reaction at a given Mach number, then you ease back the throttle and decrease speed. And down you go, perhaps calling for a course to steer home, back to Dunsfold airfield; and that's the end of that test flight.

Then it is the job of the Hawker team to read through the report written from the wire recorder and get any information they may want from me—if I can give it—and work out adjustments for the aircraft which they think will remedy the vibration or buffeting or whatever may occur at the Mach number at which the aircraft was being flown. If, for instance, it is tail vibration, more information may be necessary before adjustments are made; and the next time I go up vibrographs are placed inside the tail to get measurements of the vibration on a film.

My job, at this stage then, is to continue taking the Hunter up to 40,000-odd feet and keep on flying it until the time comes when it is moving at maximum level speed at full power in a perfectly normal manner—a nice smooth and easy flight. There are now no adverse Mach number characteristics up to maximum level flight; but we still have not reached the speed of sound. So the next thing to do is to start a series of slight dives to increase speed and Mach number, and to go through the whole process again of making a note of any troubles; and having them ironed out by the design team. Without being technical, the time came last April when I was flying in steeper dives with the Mach number getting round to 1; and realizing that I must be nearing the speed of sound but not being quite sure of it, because, due to position errors, the Machmeter may not read true at near-sonic velocity. So little is known of effects likely to occur at transonic speed that great care is required when exploring these regions of high speed.

Now you can see why, on the day the supersonic bang was heard at Ball's Cross, I had not known I had reached such a speed until Frank Bullen told me what he had learned.

This bang, or explosion, is a sure indication that an aircraft has flown at sonic speed. In fact, every time an aircraft passes through the sound barrier, it appears to cause two or more bangs.

The pilot does not hear these bangs, but on the ground you hear up to three. The steeper the angle at which an aircraft flies at a sonic speed, the smaller is the area over which the bang or explosion is heard. If the dive is fairly steep the explosion may be heard for about two miles on either side of the track of the aircraft, and may spread, say, for about five miles in length. If the angle of the dive is about thirty degrees then the distance covered in a line by the explosion may be about twenty miles or more. On one occasion a bang was heard in a line all the way from Camberley to Henley.

I knew that sooner or later we should cause these bangs; and the first were, in fact, heard over a wide area, as Frank Bullen soon got to learn when he dropped into the local at Ball's Cross, "The Stag". They had echoed all round Petworth, and the story goes that one country police-man was not too pleased. The gossip at "The Stag" was that he had been feeding his chickens in the fowl-run at the time:

"One moment there all the chooks were, pecking away. Next moment, there they all wasn't . . . they were all blown up in one corner with feathers all over the place, and me lying in the middle of the fowl-run on me back."

It may have happened, but as a rule, apart from the bangs making you jump they don't normally have much other effect. Some people have told me that they have noticed their trouser legs flapping a bit, and loose windows rattling, but that is about all. The actual pressure waves generated at present are quite weak.

Somehow, despite all the work we had put in on the Hunter, I found it a little difficult to appreciate that I had actually flown faster than the speed of sound—it seemed too easy!

Gwen, my wife, and I chatted over Frank's news in our cottage, just off the perimeter track of Dunsfold aerodrome, and I remember we had a smile that evening comparing my latest flight with my first ever.

I was about ten years old at the time; and standing in a Kent farm field, I paid great wealth—five shillings!—to go up in an Avro 504K, designed during the First World War. It puttered round in a circuit, and I was back and down on the ground before I had sufficient time to realize what flying was like.

CHAPTER 2

# *Early Flights*

I CAN still remember the smell of Castrol R fuel—so rare these days—from the rotary engine of that old Avro, the blast of cold air as we took off; and the sight below of primroses and wooded slopes.

It was Easter time, and I was staying with my Uncle Bill on his farm near Small Hythe, not very far from our home at Tonbridge. All my life my father and mother have lived at Tonbridge, Kent. My father grew up in Tonbridge, and is a Kentish man; my mother is the daughter of a Northumberland farmer who left Glanton to come south on the advice of his doctor, farmed for some thirty years just outside Tonbridge and lived to be ninety-one, an age I hope to better! I used to spend many of my school holidays, particularly in the summer, with Uncle Bill; and I was greatly excited that Easter time when we learned that two Avros had landed in a field at Pick Hill, between Tenterden and Small Hythe, to take up passengers for joy rides.

Aeroplanes and flying were one of my main hobbies, the others being ships and the sea. Looking back, it seems that as long as I can remember anything I have always been interested in aircraft and boats and ships. It may have been that my first interest in flying came from watching aircraft passing over Tonbridge on the way to Croydon or from Croydon to Paris and the Continent. I used to watch them go across the sky day by day until the time came when I could spot a Handley Page Hannibal, an Argosy, a Scylla; and German Junkers, Dutch Fokkers, Swiss DC2's, and many other types such as the DH Dragon, the Moth, the Puss Moth.

With the Royal Air Force stations, Biggin Hill and Kenley, not far away from Tonbridge, I soon learned to recognize Bristol Bulldogs, Hawker Furies and Gloster Gauntlets; as well as Hart trainers from the training school at Rochester. When air exercises took place the sky would be filled with Virginia and Heyford bombers, and perhaps Hart light bombers too; and when they were intercepted over the Tonbridge area by fighters I could not be kept indoors.

My interest in boats and then ships came from many happy hours on the river Medway, which flows through Tonbridge. If I could not go out in a boat I would walk along by the river and think about going to sea or learning to fly.

I began to collect photographs and drawings of aircraft and stick them on the walls of my bedroom; and when I was seven I began to make my first model aircraft and was so satisfied with the result that I was soon spending most of my spare time making models. Eventually I had sixty or seventy and a model aerodrome, built to scale and complete in most details. It had hangars and aircraft, petrol wagons, ambulances, and fire-engines. There were also parachutes with men on them and they floated down from the ceiling quite realistically. Outside the hangars were sand and material that looked like grass on which a number of cars were parked.

With some other boys of my age, Peter Chapman and Ivan Vickers, both of whom were to join the RAF, Leonard Edmondson, who went into Naval Aviation, and a fat boy named Billy Bateman, I formed a "Skybird Club". We all used to spend hours making models, playing with the model aerodrome, and building up quite a library of books and magazines about flying. We read all we could about the great aviators of the day—Hubert Broad, Alan Cobham, James Mollison, Jean Batten, Amy Johnson, Pauline Gower, and all the Schneider Cup pilots.

We also used to make models of ships and had a small naval library too; and when we were not working on our models we would all bicycle off together to Biggin Hill, to West Malling, Croydon, Penshurst—in fact anywhere at all to see aircraft. We used to stand and watch them and point out to each other their chief characteristics and generally air our knowledge like all small boys keen on a hobby.

We were delighted when a Hannibal force-landed after engine failure in a field near Tonbridge. And when a Miles Hawk came down in a field near Higham Lane I took the day off from the Convent school I was attending at that time and joined in helping the pilot to drag the aircraft down a slope to a flat piece of ground so that he could take off again. He got into the air all right, but then he really did crash in a wood—and I arrived home to find my absence from school had made me rather unpopular. After attending the Convent school for three years, until I was eight, I went on to Judd's School where I was a day boy and stayed until I was about seventeen and a half. I was not an outstanding pupil, but I enjoyed it on the whole, particularly the gymnasium.

I was always happy to go out to my Uncle Bill's farm for the long holidays and the good Kent earth, even though it took me away from my models. I have many happy memories of my days at Small Hythe, but none more exciting than of that first flight.

"Couple of aeroplanes landed near Pick Hill," my uncle announced one day. "They're going to take people up for rides."

I was on my bicycle and away down to that field as fast as I could go with all the pocket money I could lay my hands on. It was raining and there was a lot of low cloud about but I would have gone, quite probably, even if a blizzard had been blowing.

After standing around for a while and finding out the form I parted willingly with five shillings, which was just about all I had, and waited for my turn to go up. The Avro 504K seemed a wonderful machine with its rotary engine clop-clopping round, its wing tip skids and a long skid between the main wheels extending well forward to prevent the aircraft from nosing over. It had two cockpits, the one at the rear taking two passengers. Who worried because it had no windscreens!

I stared hard at the pilot and noted everything about him. He seemed a being apart to be able to fly an aeroplane; but yet he appeared to be casual about everything. He had a ruddy, cheerful face, rather weather-beaten from flying for years in an open cockpit and he was probably sick to death of small boys and circuits.

At last my turn came. With another ten-year-old boy I clambered into the cockpit, tense with excitement, trying not to stick my feet through the fabric-covered fuselage. We settled ourselves in, grinning at one another.

"OK?" shouted the pilot.

"Yes," we piped.

The engine seemed to roar, and a blast of cold air swept over us taking our breath away. We peeped over the sides of the cockpit; we were flying all right and there were the woods and the primroses. All too soon we were down again, bumping over the field, swinging round, clambering out, back on the grass. It had been wonderful and I felt that never had five shillings been spent so well—yet, if only I had another five shillings.

I could not tear myself away but stayed and watched flight after flight, circuit after circuit, thrilled by the memory of my experience, envious of the lucky ones now going up. While I was watching yet another take-off, I noticed a lady walking over to me; and to my surprise she spoke to me.

"I would so like to have a flight, but I have nobody to come up with me. Would you like to come with me?"

I looked up to see a lady about my mother's age and with a pleasant, smiling face; evidently she knew all about the longings of small boys.

"Yes, rather—er, yes please. And thank you very much."

Fancy anybody not wanting to go up alone! But thank goodness she wanted company.

And so there I was with her, back in the cockpit, smiling, excited, hanging on, blasted again by cold air, enjoying every second; up, round, down and out again all far too quickly.

"Thank you very much indeed," I remembered to say; and was rather puzzled by the amusement that seemed to mingle with her smile.

Two flights in one day. It seemed too good to be true; and from that time onwards pocket money had a greater meaning and significance. Odd jobs that brought in extra pence were welcome; and every time I could amass the wealth of five shillings, which was all too seldom, I scoured the countryside for joy-riding aircraft.

Sir Alan Cobham's circus was at its peak during those years, and from time to time I went up in his aircraft from other Kentish fields, from Penshurst, from the Old Barn at Hildenborough, and appetite grew with feeding. Once I went up from the Old Barn in an Airspeed Ferry, a vastly superior aircraft to the Avro, I felt. It actually carried six passengers. With careful management I got myself a seat as near the pilot as possible and felt a surge of pleasure as he pointed out for me a number of interesting things such as landmarks and other aircraft flying around. But the greatest thrill of all during that flight was to pass right over Tonbridge and to see it from the air for the first time. This was really flying.

Yet another flight was in a cockpit which had no seat. I stood clutching the rim, practically blinded by the slipstream closing my eye-lids, unable to see more than a blur of trees as we took off and landed; but it was still worth every penny of five shillings.

At the age of ten the years pass slowly and there were periods when it seemed that aeons would drag before I was sufficiently old either to learn to fly myself or to go to sea. I should have to wait until I was eighteen before I could join the RAF but I could get into the Royal Navy or the Merchant Navy, as a cadet, at only sixteen to seventeen. Flying attracted me more strongly than the sea; but supposing I failed the medical examination? At eighteen I should be too old for acceptance as a cadet. Life seemed very difficult.

My enthusiasm for the sea mounted with two trips abroad during school holidays—to Norway and to Denmark; on each occasion I took in every detail of the ship during the crossings, exulted in the life and colour and movement of the sea, forgetting temporarily about aircraft and flying. I was now about fourteen or fifteen and fired by the experiences of my voyages I wrote letters to most of the shipping companies in Leadenhall Street asking what my chances might be of joining their fleets. I received about thirty answers; but they all said the same thing—there were no vacancies for cadets for the time being. Life seemed full of disappointments.

I sounded out my headmaster, Mr. Lloyd Morgan, a learned and patient man, and discovered that both careers met with his approval, though once he observed, perhaps unimpressed by my homework, that probably the only thing I would ever fly would be a bicycle. Yet he was most helpful and encouraging and reminded me that no doubt my father and mother had plans for my future. They, however, were inclined to think that my enthusiasm for aircraft and ships was probably a boyish fad which would pass. They appreciated more than I did at the time, that if I were to go to Cranwell, the Royal Air Force College, or to Dartmouth, the Royal Naval College, a good deal of money would be required for my education. Like sensible parents, they did not want me to begin a career merely because I had made a hobby of the air and the sea and then finally to abandon it. They felt that it would be much better, for instance, if I joined a firm of auctioneers and became an articled clerk. I dreaded the idea. At the same time I sensed that if they appreciated that I was determined to fly or to go to sea they would not stand in my way. In my impatience to get a decision I decided to take things into my own hands.

One evening—about eight o'clock—when I knew my father was still in his office, I went to a telephone kiosk. I asked for his number.

"I would like to speak to Mr Duke," I said, disguising my voice as best I could.

"This is Mrs Duke here. Shall I fetch my husband?"

I had not bargained on my mother being in the office.

"Oh no. It's quite all right."

"Who is speaking?"

"I am Mr Lloyd Morgan's private secretary," I said, hoping mother would not detect my voice. "I wanted to speak to you about your son. I understand that he wants to take up flying as a career or to go to sea. I wondered what you felt about it."

"Well," said my mother, "if he is really keen on either we should not stand in his way. Just a minute. Here is my husband."

I heard them whispering. And then my father said:

"Good evening."

"Who is speaking please?"

I went through my piece again.

My father asked:

"What sort of boy is he at school?" In for a penny—

"Oh, a jolly good chap," I said.

"And do you think he would get on all right?"

"Oh yes. He has lots of ambition. I think he would get on well, especially if he took up flying."

The long and the short of it was that I discovered that father and mother would not stand in my way. I thanked them, put down the receiver, and bolted back home to be there before they returned.

But it is not easy to take in parents! Mother thought it was odd that the private secretary to the headmaster should ring my father's office at eight o'clock at night. She rang the exchange and found that my call had come from a kiosk.

"That was Neville, I'm sure," she told my father, I was settled down snugly, reading before a warm fire, when they got home.

"It's no good, Neville," said mother. "You've chosen the wrong day. It's not April the first today."

We had a good laugh; and I think we all felt happier about my future.

I realize now the justification for their concern. They were always so good and both Peggy, my sister, and I had a very happy childhood.

Time passed so slowly, but I was now determined to fly and I roamed far and wide on my bicycle to see and to watch aircraft. I was always at Biggin Hill for Empire Air Days and frequently over at Rochester staring at the Reserve Flying School "Tutors" and Harts. In 1938 I went to the opening of Gatwick Airport and there I saw Hawker Furies; they came from 43 Squadron and, tied together, did some excellent aerobatics. I was tremendously impressed by these aircraft and also by new types then coming into service with the general expansion of the RAF—Wellesleys, Wellingtons, Battles, Lysanders and Hurricanes of 3 Squadron. There were thrills in plenty for me that day: Clem Sohn did his "birdman" stunts and nearly came to grief (he was killed during his next display in France), and Al Williams, a famous American stunt pilot, performed in his highly-polished Grumman Gulfhawk. I even touched this Gulfhawk in the hangar after the display for, as usual, I had stayed on after the flying was ended to see all I could of the aircraft and hoping to be allowed to lend a helping hand. I joined in pushing the Gulfhawk into a hangar.

One day at West Malling I asked for a job in the hangars only to be refused firmly but kindly. During a visit to London with my mother I saw an aircraft on display in a shop window, urged her to enter the shop with me and somehow managed to persuade one of the attendants to let me sit in the cockpit; and it may have been on this visit that, with sixteen shillings to spend, my mother took me to a large store. There I became rooted in front of a flying model, and though she suggested that my pocket-money might be spent to better advantage and we walked all round the store inspecting possible alternatives, my mind was made up. It was the flying model or nothing. In the weeks to come it made many successful sorties, launched from my bedroom window.

Eventually the time came for me to leave Judd's School; it was the summer of 1939 and I was seventeen and a half and I was determined that when I was eighteen, on January 11th, 1940, I would go to the Air Ministry and try for a short service commission. But there were six long months to wait and, as I could not spend my time idly, I became a junior clerk in the firm of Neve and Sons, auctioneers and estate agents. I took a course at a technical school to brush up my maths for it seemed certain that I should want good maths in the RAF.

During the summer of 1939 I learned that the Royal Navy had a special entry scheme for boys of my age to train for the Fleet Air Arm. Ships and aircraft! This was what I wanted. I went before a selection board of Admirals and returned home quite hopeful; but when the war began no more entries were accepted and the scheme was abandoned. I was distressed and most unhappy; Ivan Vickers was already in the RAF,

Leonard Edmondson was in the Royal Navy. I felt odd man out. But the war had started and so I applied to enlist in the RAF immediately, only to be told I was too young. Would time never pass? And would the war still be on when I was eighteen? It was!

The "phoney" war dragged on, my work as junior clerk could not have impressed my employers favourably, Christmas passed. And then came my eighteenth birthday. I asked Neve's for the day off to travel to the RAF recruiting centre in Brighton which covered our area at Tonbridge. The train chugged along—too slowly—and eventually I arrived at the centre with a number of other volunteers. The medical examination brought no complications but when I applied to join as aircrew it was rather different.

"We can take nobody to train as a pilot or as an air observer," I was told.

"You may join as wireless operator-airgunner. Are you interested in that?"

"Only as a last resort. I want to be a pilot."

"If you became a wireless operator it is quite likely that you could train as a pilot later on."

I was still not keen, and perhaps my insistence on wanting to become a pilot had some effect. If that was so I was fortunate for several people got caught that way. John Derry, although he wanted to be a pilot, joined as a wireless operator-airgunner and it was some long time before he was able to change.

Yet whatever I wanted to be I still had to wait. I was told that I would not be called up for some time—"an indefinite period". How indefinite it seemed as I went back to junior clerking, a little more satisfied, a little less restless, still wanting time to pass.

It passed with Dunkirk. At Tonbridge railway station I saw the gallant survivors going by in trains, and lent a hand in helping to get wounded men to the hospitals in Tunbridge Wells. The sight of some of the wounded was disturbing at my age, but at least I knew that I was doing something positive.

And then at last in the middle of June 1940, there came a note from the Air Ministry telling me to report at Uxbridge for an interview before a selection board which would approve me—or not—for aircrew as pilot.

"As pilot." That was the best news yet. I got another day off from the office; and at Uxbridge there were one or two tricky moments before the selection board, but I was able to prove that my maths were of sufficient standard. The medical examination was very stiff and I worried in case I failed; my pulse rate seemed quite excessive but I told myself that allowance would be sure to be made for this.

Then back to Tonbridge, another period of waiting—and finally a note telling me to report to Uxbridge. I was in the RAF at last, the lowest form of life—AC2. But the grandest title I could imagine: AC2, Pilot, U/T.

Now that the time came to leave home I felt the wrench of saying good-bye to my father and mother and to Peggy. The longest period I had been away from them so far had been during the school holiday fortnights in Norway and Denmark. We had been a very close circle and now we could not be sure when we should all be together again. With my mother, I wrapped up all my books and magazines that I had collected over the years; we covered the aircraft models and the aerodrome with a dust sheet.

"Where are you off to this time, young sir?" the clerk at the booking office at Tonbridge station asked, eyeing my suitcase.

"He's going to Uxbridge to join the RAF," said Peggy.

"Hope he learns to fly better than he can play cricket, miss."

The RAF Depot at Uxbridge was an impersonal, bustling place and there were many like myself in sports coat and flannels, most of us curious, slightly reserved, feeling rather strange. We were not there for long.

Our first move was to Padgate, near Liverpool, where we were fitted out with uniforms, and with my height the expected happened. Trousers were either too short and too narrow round the waist, or too long and too wide round the waist; the jacket fitted where it touched, and the boots seemed to be made of lead. The only things that suited me were: knife, fork, spoon, button-cleaner and polishing stick.

From Padgate we went—with pleasure—to Bexhill and to No. 4 Initial Training Wing, arriving just in time to help to move the wing to Paignton, in Devon. It seemed a fell plot to delay my first flight. We lived in the Hydro Hotel and while part of the routine was to take lectures on RAF organization and subjects like elementary navigation, we spent long hours drilling, marching, and getting ourselves fit with physical training for the flying training course. And when the time came to move on to No. 13 Elementary Flying Training School at White Waltham we were pretty fit, our only preoccupation being whether we should make the grade.

This was it at last, we felt as we got to White Waltham. Now we became LAC Pilot U/T and our pay increased magnificently to about fourteen shillings a week. We lived in army-type wooden huts, and I was made Acting Corporal (unpaid) with the responsibility of seeing that our hut was kept clean and tidy and the Course marched in an orderly and proper manner to lectures and to flying.

White Waltham had been one of the De Havilland flying schools and it was now the home of the newly-formed Air Transport Auxiliary which ferried new aircraft from factories to squadrons. For the first time we saw a Spitfire, as well as many other new types; I had a very careful look at this Spitfire and hardened my preference to become a fighter pilot. But, first of all, came training on Tiger Moths.

We were allotted to various flying instructors and the man who taught me to fly was Flying Officer Rea. He was a magnificent instructor, patient, quiet, kindly. I have never forgotten him and I owe a tremendous amount to him, a massive, tall man with a face weather-beaten from flying in Tiger Moths for years. Another instructor was Merrick Hymans, whom I was to meet again.

We were issued with a log book and I was pleased and perhaps a little self-conscious when I made my first entry:

"August 20th, 1940. Tiger Moth N6790. Pilot, P/O Thompson. Passenger, self. 1: air experience. 2: familiarity with cockpit layout. Dual, fifteen minutes."

It was purely a "look-see" first flight, from a nearby airfield, Waltham St. Lawrence, used as a satellite to White Waltham for circuits and landings. There were no five shillings to pay this time! Then followed my first instruction flight of half an hour with Flying Officer Rea. This was the life. We flew practically every day—taxiing, turning, gliding, practising take-off and landing until September 6th. On that day, while the Battle of Britain was approaching its climax, I flew three times at White Waltham, twice doing spins to the left and to the right.

After the second flight, Rea said:

"OK, Duke. You can take her up now by yourself."

My first solo! By now I had done eight and a half hours' tuition with Rea; and I was so pleased and so busy concentrating on doing everything correctly during my first solo of ten minutes that I was not in the least worried by the empty seat in front. It was exhilarating. Two days later I flew seven times between dawn and dusk, four times solo. This was the life all right.

The Battle of Britain had been fought and won when, on September 20th, I went up for my final flight at White Waltham. My log book now recorded 20 hours 30 minutes dual flying, and 13 hours 35 minutes solo.

The course moved on to Hatfield and No. 1 EFTS until No. 5 Flying Training School at Sealand, near Chester would take us. At Sealand we learned to fly a Miles Master, a larger, faster and more advanced aircraft than the Tiger Moth, with complications of mixture and pitch controls, retractable undercarriage, and many more flying instruments. There was greater concentration on navigation, and we were launched on instrument and cross-country flying and aerobatics.

We had another move just before Christmas, this time to the Flying Training School at Tern Hill. Here I was selected as a potential officer and, in addition to the white-flash cap we had been wearing, I was given a white armband and moved into the officers' mess.

This period at Tern Hill had its moments. Two days after my nineteenth birthday I had to do an instrument flight in fairly thick weather to Leicester. With another pupil, J Booth, in the reserve seat I got the Miles Master to the right place over Leicester and carefully selected a railway line to follow back to Tern Hill. The idea was good but it was the wrong line. The clouds became thicker and thicker until neither Booth nor I could see a thing. Suddenly a dark shape loomed up. A barrage balloon. I pulled hard back on the stick and up we went, right through the balloons, missing several by what seemed to be inches, climbing through 6,000 feet of cloud, completely lost. It was a pretty lonely feeling sitting up there above the clouds without the vaguest idea of where we might be.

"That looks like a gap," Booth said after a while.

It was a gap all right, and we went down through it to find Worcester and its cathedral below. I returned to Tern Hill a little thoughtfully, and Booth also seemed rather pre-occupied. There followed more hours both day and night in the Miles Master until the second week in February 1941 when we were presented with our wings, commissioned as pilot officers, and sent off again, this time to No. 58 Operational Training Unit at Grangemouth, near Edinburgh. As the time for our posting approached I became increasingly anxious; we knew that a number of pupils would be wanted for bomber pilots, for instructors and for Army co-operation units. But I wanted to be a fighter pilot, and it was a great relief when my posting to Grangemouth came through.

So at length all the preliminaries were ended and we were to fly

Spitfires for the first time. A number of us arrived at Grangemouth, very new and raw pilot officers, rather overawed at the tough-looking and experienced instructors, all Battle of Britain men.

I flew a Spitfire I for the first time on March 2nd for twenty-five minutes and my first impression was of its very long nose and its terrific take-off speed of about 85 miles per hour! It cruised at 240 miles per hour compared with the 180 miles per hour of the Miles Master. It was a nice aircraft to fly, easy to handle, except for one thing: you had to pump with the right hand to get the undercarriage up, with the result that you tended to pitch fore and aft following take-off, due to the very light elevator control.

The Spitfire I could also be a bit awkward for beginners to land. I overshot on one landing, but felt that I could get down quite all right without opening the throttle and going round again. But I couldn't. The machine went off the runway and tipped up on its nose.

It was a most embarrassing moment. Up roared a fire tender and an ambulance; before they arrived there was an awful few minutes of dead silence, broken only by the hiss of the gyros still spinning. I felt a complete clot perched up in the cockpit; and I was left in little doubt that I was one, in fact. Aircraft were still scarce and every single one was badly needed after the Battle of Britain; mine now required a new airscrew. Unfortunately, I was not the only offender: there were several prangs and collisions, and a number of pupils did not survive the course.

We were at Grangemouth for about six weeks, practising formation flying, dog-fighting, aerobatics, instrument flying; making mock attacks, and firing our machine guns on exercises. And then at the end of March we were ready to be posted to operational squadrons. I had a grand total of 145 hours 50 minutes flying time, including 26 hours 10 minutes in the Spitfire I.

We were asked which squadrons we should like to join, though the choice was pretty limited. There was only one place I had in mind: Biggin Hill. It held so many memories for me, and it was now one of the star Battle of Britain stations, right in the war. Furthermore, it was No. 11 Group of Fighter Command, the RAF's front line in 1941.

I plumped hard to be sent to Biggin, and after some persuasion managed to get the posting together with Gordon Brettell, who had trained with me from FTS onwards. Both of us felt pretty operational and ready to take on any of these German chaps.

We were soon to find out how little we really knew.

## CHAPTER 3

# *Biggin Hill in 1941*

BIGGIN HILL was still very much of a Battle of Britain casualty in April 1941. It had received every kind of attention from the Luftwaffe; there was not a hangar standing intact; walls were smashed all over the station; and it seemed that there was hardly a window in one piece. There was mud, oceans of it, wherever you went. Yet to me it was still the same old Biggin I had known as a youngster on Empire Air Days, and it was wonderful to drive up to the mess in a car knowing that I had come to stay and to fly with a Squadron instead of making a brief day-visit.

At that time Biggin was commanded by Group Captain "Mongoose" Soden, and its wing was led by Wing Commander "Sailor" Malan, DSO, DFC, who had already become a name in Fighter Command and who could fly a Spitfire to its limit and get the last ounce out of it. The squadrons forming the wing were: No. 92 (East India), commanded by Squadron Leader Jamie Rankin, DSO, DFC, a Scot with wonderful eyesight; No. 74, commanded by Squadron Leader Mungo Park, DFC, and No. 609 commanded by Squadron Leader Robinson, DFC, who also formed a Belgian flight in it. Both were later killed in combat.

I was to join 92 Squadron and to go to B Flight, commanded by Flight Lieutenant Alan Wright, DFC. Flight Lieutenant Brian Kingcome, DSO, DFC, whom I was to get to know very well over the years, commanded A flight. 92 had a terrific spirit. It was top-scoring squadron in No. 11 Group with one hundred and thirty-five enemy aircraft destroyed. All the pilots were magnificent chaps, many of them pre-war regulars or short-service men, and most of them had taken part in the Battle of Britain. They included Flight Sergeant Don Kingaby, who won three DFM's before he was commissioned, Flight Sergeant "Titch" Havercroft, DFM, an extremely small pilot and one of the most gallant and cheerful; Flying Officers Tommy Lund and Roy Mottram, "Babe" Whittamore, Peter Humphreys, and "Tommy" Thompson. Tommy was my room-mate; he was an enormous man and a former Public Schools heavyweight champion. He took a deep pride in a much-tattered uniform, and was kind and almost fatherly to new boys such as myself. He was killed several years later while flying in Transport Command. Others I remember were the Station "Spy" or Intelligence Officer, De La Torre; the Squadron "Spy", Tommy Weisse, a Norwegian, who, like all Intelligence Officers, were usually entirely unmoved by excitable tales of combats; and Squadron Leader Bill Igo, one of the controllers—the Biggin controllers were adept at getting us mixed up in successful trouble with the Jerries.

I arrived to join 92 with Gordon Brettell, a quiet, likeable chap, later to be shot down over France, taken prisoner, and sent to Stalag Luft 3. He took part in the celebrated mass escape and was one of those shot after Hitler had a fit of carpet-biting. Gordon and I were the first of the wartime-trained pilots to go to the squadron, and not unnaturally we were regarded with a good deal of curiosity.

I have never forgotten the friendliness and kindness shown to Gordon and me during those first days with 92. We were both pretty young—I was now only nineteen and a couple of months—and a bit shy and nervous; but nobody seemed to hold that against us, chatting away to our questions and giving us all the tips they possibly could.

"Come and have a noggin at the White Hart," some of them asked us at the end of our first day.

The White Hart, at Brasted, near Westerham, was run during the war by Mrs Kathleen Preston while her husband was away serving with the Royal Navy. It has a wonderful, low-ceilinged bar with roof timbers taken from old sailing ships, and is several hundred years old. Kath gave the Biggin Hill squadrons the freedom of the place; she was a great friend to everyone and none of us ever forgot her. We spent many contented hours there, relaxing after strenuous ops, and a number of the pilots signed their names in chalk on a blackboard that had been used for a black-out curtain. It hangs at the RAF Museum, Hendon.

That first night, Gordon and I helped to consume a suitable quantity of liquor and in due course removed ourselves to bed.

I was keen to find out everything about the Spitfires the squadron was flying. They were mark 5's, with two cannons, four machine guns, new

Merlin engines which were giving a bit of teething-trouble; and a new hood-release to help you get rid of the canopy if you had to bale out. They could climb like monkeys and get up comfortably to 38,000 feet. Even so, the Jerries could still climb above us, and it seemed that they were always above and behind. 92 squadron was the first to get 20 mm cannons, and for a start we frequently had trouble with stoppages. We were also given metal instead of fabric ailerons; they made the aircraft much more manoeuvrable at high speed, and marked a turning-point in the use of the Spitfire. Gordon and I absorbed all this gen eagerly.

"Now come along to my briefing room," Tommy Weisse said to us.

He took us to his office, where we pored over maps and photographs of Jerry airfields in France—and how well we were to get to know France. Somehow, because of the German fighters, it seemed always to have a sinister look to me, and even now I get memories of Messerschmitts and Focke Wulfs whenever I see it from the air.

"Now to the crew room," said Tommy.

Every fighter pilot will remember his first glimpse of a crew room. They seemed to be the same everywhere—a complete shambles at first sight; a gramophone pounding out the latest hit, a smoky old stove in the middle of the floor, usually either stone-cold or bursting with heat, flying-kit and parachutes on the walls, an untidy desk covered with flying orders, gramophone records, technical books on the Spitfire engine and airframe, a notice-board smothered with notices showing the squadron's state of readiness, pilot's names and the machines they were to fly and their position in their sections. And to brighten the place up a bit, coloured drawings of gorgeous popsies taken from some popular magazine and pinned up in a conspicuous spot. Sprawled around in chairs would be several pilots, on readiness. In their Mae Wests, flying-boots, and usually with coloured scarfs at their throats, they would be playing cards, perhaps chess; some chatting, others dozing.

Roy Mottram, deputy commander of B Flight, took us under his wing.

"Come on," he said. "Let's get you fixed with your 'chutes and then have a look at the ops room."

Biggin's operations room, from which all sorties were controlled, had been bombed during the Battle of Britain and was still out of commission. We went over to Keston, where a temporary one had been fixed up.

In a very short time we settled down to squadron life.

There is nothing quite like life with an operational squadron. It appealed to me immediately; and, all through the war, the happiest and most contented times I spent were during my three tours. The squadron spirit, the strong sense of fellowship with everyone bound together by the common dangers and the love of flying, the feeling that you are at last doing something definite, the thrill of flying, and, at the back of your mind, the realization that your life may not only be eventful but also short—all these things combine to make you live with a certain amount of gusto.

You not only admire the men you fly with, but you become attached to them. Though you realize that some time you may be shot down, yet at the back of your mind you always feel that it won't really happen to you—it may happen to others, but not to you. Periods of intense action when you become so tired that you act almost automatically are alternated with periods of inactivity and excruciating boredom. But always there is the corporate sense of the squadron-in-being. And there is always a zest for parties, when you drink because you are excited or elated; or because you are tired and scared; or because you want to forget for the moment that one of the chaps has been shot down. You like to know a number of pretty girls, but when you are nineteen or in your early twenties you don't particularly want to be too serious with any of them, for one thing because you are too young to marry and for another—well, you can't see so very far ahead in war. Not much further than the next sortie.

Somehow or other you slip easily into this atmosphere until you feel that you have never lived any other kind of life. And then, suddenly, you realize you want a change; the strain of operations, the effects of pro-longed nervous tension time and time again, make you want a rest. And then, having realized you are tired, you won't admit it to yourself and you begin to fight any suggestion from any quarter that you need a rest. Finally, when you are ordered away, you want to be back again with your own squadron after a week or less. Gordon and I were keen to start operational flying.

"Better do a sector reconnaissance first," Jamie Rankin told us. "There's an old Spitfire I you can take up and have a look around the place."

I went up for my first flight at Biggin on April 7th 1941 and my log book shows that I spent an hour and a quarter scouting around. It was not altogether a joy ride, for even during training flights we were armed up and had to keep a sharp look-out for Jerries. A few days later, after an instructive radio-telephone course at Uxbridge, I went up in my first Spitfire V. And life was very good.

Then came the day Gordon and I had been waiting for—our first operation.

"Scramble to patrol Dungeness area."

And up we went with Pilot Officer Ronny Fokes and Don Kingaby. A "scramble" meant that you had been waiting on readiness, all kitted-up ready for flying, with the aircraft set for immediate take-off. If not on readiness you were either on thirty minutes or fifteen minutes "available", which meant that you had to be ready to go to dispersal within that period if you were called on. For a scramble, the aircraft took off singly, and formed up in the air; but for a set operation, such as a sweep, they took off in twelves.

We scrambled for my first op.

It was not very exciting. The four of us climbed to 35,000 feet over the Channel, were directed on to some Jerries, but never saw them. Anyway, I fired my cannons on test over Beachy Head and went home feeling a little less like a new boy.

Things were a bit quiet round about that time, and all the flying I got for the next few days was practising formation, aerobatics, attacks and dogfighting. Once or twice I flew over to have a look at Tonbridge and Tenterden for a mild beat up.

During the middle of April Mr Churchill came to Biggin, and his visit put everybody on their toes. It was my first glimpse of the great man, and I remember seeing him in the distance.

A different experience was my first squadron celebration party.

"Jamie Rankin and Bruinier got a 109 this morning." Gordon told me. "It's the CO's first blood."

Bruinier was one of our Netherlands East Indies boys, and a Flight Lieutenant. With Jamie he had scrambled in fairly dirty weather and sighted a Messerschmitt 109 over Dungeness. Apparently the 109 had been machine-gunning Rye, and when its pilot saw the two Spitfires he obviously mistook them for friends. He made no attempt to duck into cloud, but even waggled his wings at them. A bad mistake! He went down in flames, baled out, and was taken prisoner.

I forget what time the party began, but I know some nurses came over from Orpington Hospital, and we got cracking at the White Hart. I remember taking the nurses back to Orpington, getting back to Biggin and bed at 4 a.m. and staying there until 11.30 a.m., thankful that there was no dawn readiness and no flying that day.

Finally, and before April was out, I really did fire my guns at a Jerry for the first time.

"Nine aircraft, squadron sweep at maximum height. Take-off 1300 hours," Ronny Fokes told us. I was one of the nine.

Biggin slipped behind; Ronny Fokes was leading, and soon we heard the controller on the r/t.

"Bogeys at angels three zero"—a "bogey" was an unidentified aircraft. These turned out to be Hurricanes, and we veered away, over the Channel again.

Then we saw seven 109's, a few hundred feet below us, in pairs. I can still see them. They looked like a line of little rats, or mice, and when they saw us it was just as though they were bolting for their holes! They nosed straight over and into a vertical dive as we caught them up.

Ronny Fokes was in front, I was on his left and Roy Mottram was on his right, with the rest of the formation spread out behind—all of us leaving thick ropes of vapour trail behind. I picked a 109, and got astern and slightly to port just as he put his nose down to dive for home. I fired a short burst and was sure of a hit because a flash of flame came from his engine on the port side. But I was unable to follow down as another Spitfire came between us, and went down after him.

Frankly, I was terrifically excited and elated; and later on that evening I jotted down my feelings in my diary. Here they are, for what they're worth:

It is hard to remember your feelings and thoughts in a fight, especially your first. I don't think there is any feeling of fear, just an excited urge with a queer little feeling inside and the thought that you must get closer and closer. Knowing you have friends along with you helps more than anything else, I think. Perhaps your pulse beats faster, and it is a little hard to breathe; and although it is all over in a few seconds you feel very tired but with a queer feeling of elation inside you. This, I think, is because you know that the machine you have just fired at is your enemy and that he would shoot at you and kill you, if he could. I know I was not afraid, but very wary. After this squirt at the 109 I was chasing my own tail and my eyes were popping out of my head looking for other enemy aircraft. Where there were a dozen machines a few seconds ago, now there are none. Neither friend, nor foe. The sky seems empty. It's uncanny.

Coming home you try to remember what has happened. Did you hit him? You must have hit him. You couldn't have missed. Soon you are convinced in your own mind that you have really shot him down. This feeling must be fought against. You might have hit him, yes, but did you see him go down? Did you see him on fire? Did you see him bale out? No, you didn't! Oh, well! Perhaps next time. You've been in action, anyway, you say. Now you can shoot a line in the mess!

On the way home you might pick up with one or two of the squadron roaring back on the deck. You come alongside and make furious gestures and beat things up—innocent things like trees and fields. Life is great! You have fired your guns in hate. Get a bit lower now; gently back on the stick and up and over that rooftop! Arriving back at the 'drome you fly slowly round the circuit. Flying slowly, you can hear the wind whistling in your gunports where you have broken the canvas patches when you fired—and so can the people on the ground. Holding off to land . . . throttle back . . . 95, 90 miles per hour . . . stick back . . . back, back, back. The whistling rises to a pitch, then slowly dies as the machine stalls on to the ground, and stops altogether as you trundle and bounce a little on this uneven green turf, and run to a stop. Look behind. Another machine is landing. Flaps up with a hiss of escaping air . . . seat up a little . . . oxygen mask undone to get some cool, unrestricted air into your lungs . . . lean out as you taxi. Taxi-ing a little fast perhaps . . . keen to tell your story . . . bursting to tell your story. There's your crew pleased to see you and their machine back and the guns fired. Blast the tail round with a noisy burst of throttle. Heave the airscrew into coarse . . . brakes on and pull the idle cut-out, stopping 1,200 horse-power with a pull of your finger. Quickly undo your straps. Steady . . . mustn't appear excited! Look as if this is nothing to you! Off comes your helmet—and you get mixed up in r/t and oxygen tubes. Blast! Turn the parachute buckle, and give it a bang . . . lower the door . . . heave yourself up by the top of the front bullet-proof glass, and swing out of the cockpit. Home again!

Yes, you reply, you did fire at something. Hit? Perhaps—don't know.

The Intelligence Officer takes it all in, but doesn't appear excited. Damn the fellow!

The other types are waiting in a bunch, all talking at once with their hands showing exactly how they did it. Oh, hell, nobody seems to think my show was exciting! But it was—I know it was!

Off comes the Mae West, the flying boots and gloves. Off to the mess to celebrate. But wait! We are not all here. It's OK. One is refuelling down on the coast at Hawkinge; he'll be here later. Pile into the brake—steerage for me, I'm very junior. Tramp into the bar. Beer, beer, beer. Voices are raised once more to tell the other people in the lesser squadrons how we did it. Nobody mentions my show. Nobody wants to hear my show! To them it wasn't exciting. But it was—I know it was. God! How it was! Later I read the Intelligence Officer's report—giving a lurid description of how Ronny Fokes's 109 went down with its prop stopped and crashed in the sea off the French coast. The report adds, "Two other Spitfires also fired." Damn that Intelligence Officer!

It is amusing to look back on those notes after all these years. I suppose that experience was shared by hundreds of other fighter pilots at some time or other; and what a mixture of emotions we went through. I remember that soon after this "do" I had my first forty-eight hours' leave. It was good to go home again to the folks at Tonbridge, and to see a number of old friends; but it was equally good to get back again, keen to fly, wondering whether you really would get some Jerries—and reflecting that they were probably having the same thoughts about us!

But it was not until the middle of June that I had my next opportunity of having another crack at a 109.

In the meanwhile I became a little more experienced. There were many wild scrambles, various turns at dawn readiness, the odd convoy patrol and sweep, more aerobatics and training, and testing cannons. And one unauthorised flight!

I flew a Magister over to Dumborne Farm, at Small Hythe, to have tea with my Uncle Bill. Landing on a small field I had to overshoot on the first approach, and then I got down by just missing some treetops.

Faces began popping over hedges, and one or two people seemed to think I had crash-landed. But it was just a social call.

Sometimes there were sweeps when everything seemed to go wrong, including one when I had to turn back because I couldn't get the oxygen working and later went into a spin for 15,000 feet completely out of control. I remember that Wimpy Wade, who was in B Flight too, and whom I was to know so well in later years, got shot up by a 109 that day.

There was the odd party or two, one or two rushes back to Biggin at midnight praying that there would be no dawn readiness next day; sweet relief at finding I could lie in bed, and a mental resolve to pack up the fast life!

Towards the end of May I did my first "Rhubarb". This was the name given to individual low-level patrols over France to study form and shoot up any rewarding targets. I went off with Monty, Lieutenant De Montbron, a Free French pilot, separating from Rankin and Kingaby at Boulogne. We crossed the coast in cloud and Monty dived at an airfield somewhere or other. I lost him, and prowled off on my own, ducking in and out of cloud at 4,000 feet. There were no Jerries about; I found no suitable targets, didn't fire a shot at anything, but coming out over the coast the ack-ack was extremely hostile and I mistook Dunkirk for Calais. Flying back at nought feet over the channel I watched my petrol gauge anxiously. There seemed miles of sea, and I was very glad to hit the coast at Harwich and to force-land at Gravesend having steered too northerly a course. I had been flying for two hours, my longest flight in a Spitfire to that time. After re-fuelling I got back to Biggin in ten minutes. Other new experiences were night flying from West Malling and acting as top escort for three Blenheims on a shipping strike which went to bomb a couple of ships off the coast of Calais. And so to my next shot at a Jerry.

On June 14th, a Saturday, two hundred fighters went up from the Biggin, Kenley, North Weald and Hornchurch wings to cover twenty-four Blenheims bombing St Omer, hotbed of 109's. The bombers were partly a bait to get the 109's up, as they seldom intercepted a fighter sweep on its own. 92 and 74 squadrons had the job of covering the Calais-Boulogne area at between 7,000 feet and 10,000 feet. Once again I jotted down my impressions—partly because I was so brassed off with myself later, and to drive home a couple of lessons I learned. Here they are:

It was a perfect summer day in England, clear and cloudless. I was

No. 2 to my flight commander Alan Wright—I was nearly always his No. 2—a grand little fellow with wiry, fair hair, short and stocky, blue eyes and a ready smile. I rather let him down this day.

How it happened, I don't quite know. I remember the first indication I had that we were engaged was something going down vertically, going like a bomb out of a clear, cloudless sky—the sun glinting on a yellow nose. Gone in a flash. But I knew what it had been—a 109. A 109 looks almost beautiful in the air; a slim, graceful thing, picturesque, and always seems to be going like a rocket. A 109 is a nasty thing to handle, though; and many is the pilot who has had a last vision of a yellow nose with a splash of red flickering in the spinner's hub . . . perhaps a glimpse of white ropes of tracer darting towards him. Yes, there's colour in a 109!

The formation broke up. Now I could see more 109 tracer, I saw Monty chasing a 109; he was leaving two trails of black smoke as he fired his cannons. But also on Monty's tail was a 109 just closing into range. I left Alan—an unforgivable thing for a No. 2 to do—and turned after their aircraft in line astern. I was too far out of range to do much, but I had to frighten that 109 on Monty's tail somehow. I pulled the nose up and round, and pressed the middle button, letting go with cannons and machine-guns. It worked. Although the shots went nowhere near the 109, he saw some of my tracer and broke away and went down.

I whirled around in the tightest circles in the world for a while. Then I saw a machine a little below me. By Gee, a 109! Down and round, cramming on the boost; but he had seen me, and he turned. I turned and opened fire, too soon. I knew I was not hitting him but I just had to fire, fool that I was. We turned a couple of times before he went on his back and heaved his stick back and went down. No good my following, he's got too many friends there. I pulled away, cussing my waste of ammo. And there before me and getting closer was the belly of a 109. I must have been going fast as I had to throttle right back to avoid overshooting him. What luck! I must have been only twenty yards astern, and tightly under his tail, rocking gently in his slipstream. He hadn't seen me. He was flying straight and level; his tail was slipping slightly from side to side; perhaps he was a bit heavy on the rudder. I lined the sights up beautifully. Steady up a bit . . . bit more. Now! I pressed the button. I pressed it again and again, harder and harder. Nothing happened! No ammunition! Oh, for Pete's sake, just a few rounds . . . just a few. That tail gently slipping from side to side . . . only a few yards from my prop.

Should I? Dare I? Just hit his elevators. I could make it home . . . or could I, with a busted prop? The English coast looked far away—too far. Now suppose this Jerry sees me here . . . how am I to leave him? He started a gentle turn to the left. I must get out of here! Stick hard over to the right . . . hard rudder, and stick back in my stomach. Down . . . down . . . vertically for the sea . . . aileron turning. He won't catch me now. Flatten out in mid-Channel with everything screaming and going like the wind, neither coast in sight. On, on, for a few minutes which seem like hours. A speck ahead. I catch it up fast. Another Spitfire— Kingaby—also going home on the deck. I form up on him in line abreast for mutual protection. A coastline appears, closer and closer. Oh, good old England. It's Dungeness . . . Dungeness where I used to play and fish as a kid.

We nip in over the coast and pass the lighthouse, gleaming black and white, and on, over the marshes to the green patchwork of fields beyond. Back to Biggin, via the Ashford line in no time.

Alan Wright had been shot up pretty badly. He did not see me leave him, and fool that I was I never told him that I was leaving. He had looked behind and seen a machine where I should have been and thought I was still there. But I wasn't. Next thing, tracer was whistling and whirling past him and he was shot up badly. He got away OK, however, and with a damaged aileron, had to crash-land at Lympne at 140 miles per hour.

I deserved a good ticking-off for leaving Alan; but he realized that I had learned my lesson and confined himself to a few carefully selected words. And I never forgot those two lessons: don't break away from your leader without telling him; don't waste your ammunition.

The weather was now first-rate for operations, warm, clear and sunny and the wing was kept pretty busy on sweeps and escorting bombers. Several in the squadron got 109's including the CO, Jamie Rankin, Wimpy Wade, Sergeant Morris; but I was having no luck. Once when we were giving top cover to Blenheims bombing near Calais two 109's dived on Alan Wright and me. They didn't engage us, but I got a good view of the glittering wings and belly of one; and of enormous black crosses as he whizzed past. I got a great kick out of leading two sections for the first time, patrolling between Dover and Dungeness, but we were quite disappointed at seeing no Jerries. And then came a day when I nearly bought it.

On June 23rd, while we were providing cover to Blenheims bombing Bethune, we were jumped on by 109's. Jamie Rankin sent one down in flames, and later got another; Phil Archer (a Canadian) and Kingaby collected two more. In the general mix up I got separated from the squadron, and I began to feel pretty lonely over Le Touquet when five Me-109 F's showed up, broke into pairs with the fifth climbing up in front of me. He came at me head-on, opening fire at long range, and I saw his guns winking and tracer going past. But he got in my sights, and I opened up with both cannons and machine-guns. He skimmed over the top of me and I had a glimpse of white and black smoke coming from his engine. Then his friends started to work on me in two pairs and I had a pretty warm time trying to dodge them all the way down to the deck. My Spitfire was hit twice in the wings by machine-gun bullets. Fortunately, they left me when we were just over the sea, and I was glad to get back to Biggin and put in my first claim—for one 109 damaged. There was another circus that evening, when I led Gordon and Archer; but we only saw one 109 which took a look at us and sheered off smartly. Sergeant Morris was shot down that day and taken prisoner in France. He lost an arm.

The following day I had another shaky do. The wing was over St Omer with Blenheims. Alan Wright and I saw two 109's; we dived at a phenomenal speed but we couldn't catch them. When they pulled up vertically I did the same and blacked out and very nearly stalled. Just in time I noticed two of their friends behind me, did a terrific turn and saw some tracer just missing! I was quite happy to find myself on my own again somewhere over Dunkirk. Looking around I saw a dog-fight going on, and joined in quickly. I found a 109 shooting at a Spit—it was Wimpy Wade beating up another Jerry—so I sat on his tail, and fired several bursts from about 150 yards. Glycol streamed out and he started going down. I flew above him and looked into the cockpit. I could see the pilot crouched over his stick. He did not look up, perhaps because I had hit him. Anyway, he went right down and crashed a few miles inland from the Dunkirk area. It was now time to go home, because my petrol was getting low and the ammo was just about used up. I remember keeping low over the sea, going at a terrific bat; and that, just as I touched down at Biggin, my engine stopped. The tanks were dry.

I was naturally pretty pleased to have got my first Jerry, particularly as I had nearly been collected myself; but a few days later I found myself in hospital at Orpington.

The trouble began with a pain in my throat; it may have been a touch of tonsilitis or a cold. I suppose I should not have flown until I had got the thing cleared up; but there was a sweep on over the Channel and I wanted to go. Two 109's got on my tail and I put the Spit into a half roll and a steep dive. As I went down I felt a most excruciating pain in my ears. It was so intense that, once I had levelled out, I took off my helmet to try to clear my ears and was shocked to find that I could no longer hear the engine. At Hawkinge, landing to refuel, I could hear nothing that was said to me and began to worry in case my ears were damaged seriously.

In fact, my ear drums were cracked. The doc packed me off to hospital, and to my great relief, my hearing gradually returned. It was another lesson learned: don't fly on operations unless you are one hundred per cent fit.

I had a week's leave after coming out of hospital; but it all meant a gap of three weeks before I flew again.

CHAPTER 4

# War over France

IT was good to be back at Biggin again with 92. I was keen to catch up with all the news.

"Sailor Malan had a bar to his DSO, Brian Kingcome a bar to his DFC, and Wimpy Wade has the DFC," Peter Humphreys, whom we usually called "Hunk", told me. "Alan Wright has finished his tour and has been posted and Tommy Lund has got B Flight."

Unfortunately, there had been some losses, two pilots having been shot down in flames, and two more had gone into the sea but had been picked up. I was the more pleased to hear of their rescue for one of them had been wearing my helmet! One or two other chaps had been posted; I was becoming relatively senior. Indeed I was no longer the new boy of three-and-a-half months ago, and had learned sufficient to appreciate how much more I had to learn; sufficient, also, to realize that the life of a fighter pilot was strenuous at times, and that if your chances of survival depended a lot on skill you also needed more than an ounce of luck.

For a few days after my return things were fairly quiet, and I was able to ease back into operations again comfortably.

"When the Wingco flies with us, I want you to be his Number 2," Jamie Rankin told me in the crew room one morning.

This was quite an experience, and from Sailor Malan and Don Kingaby, too, I learned a great deal. Neither man was easy to stay with. Though Sailor flew steadily while he was leading the Wing, it was a different thing once the usual whirl of dog-fighting began. More than once I was so preoccupied with keeping on his tail and with looking around and behind for 109's that I did not know that he was on the tail of a Jerry himself. Once I suddenly found myself flying through bits of a 109 before I even realized that he had fired his guns and once he showered me with spent cartridge cases and links, which was awkward,

47

for they were known to crack hoods, pierce radiators and damage airscrews.

Neither Sailor nor Don flew straight and level for a second once they became separated from the main body of the squadron. They were masters in the air, and got everything out of their aircraft; with Sailor especially, it was full throttle work most of the time. From such men as these I soon learned to weave and to search the sky continuously, never relaxing until we had landed.

Stirling bombers were now beginning to be used for daylight raids; they usually flew in threes, escorted by Spitfires. We were quite impressed by seeing their numerous bombs bursting during a raid on Lille. We were also impressed, but in a different way, when we saw a Stirling hit by ack-ack. Sometimes we escorted torpedo-Beauforts on anti-shipping sorties. An eventful day began when we flew with six Beauforts as they beat up a tanker, which was supported by E-boats, off Fécamp. That was during the morning; in the afternoon I provided top-cover for nine Blenheims bombing Hazebrouck marshalling yards— and I was very glad—and a bit relieved—when I got down again.

We were at 25,000 feet and there were lots of 109's about; too many, in fact, and one of them got on my tail and I saw his tracer going just over my hood. I got out of his way by turning hard and climbing, only to be jumped on by eight of his friends. I used all the dodges I could and managed to get away from them when I was well out to sea. To add insult to injury I was then attacked by a Spitfire. This was a rather suspicious attack, for the Spitfire used typical German head-on and half-roll away tactics. Back at Biggin I took off again for the third trip that day, this time escorting a Lysander looking for one of our pilots in the sea off North Foreland. The weather was misty and it was difficult to maintain contact with a slow flying Lysander. We saw nothing.

"Let's have a party," Tommy Lund said to me that evening.

With Brian Kingcome we went over to the "White Hart" for a few drinks and met some girl friends before going on to a Sergeant's Mess dance. It was good to relax like this, and to forget the doings of the afternoon; but I must admit that I was a bit tired when I got back to Biggin early next morning.

This time I was on dawn readiness. And on this occasion I found little to commend getting up in the dark on a July day; but it was typical of wartime fighter operations, and how many times it happened! Sweeps at dawn were a good time for finding the Jerry on a shipping and weather recce; but during the flight that morning, after I had taken off at 8 a.m. on my own to patrol between Ostend and Cap Gris Nez, I only saw an E-boat and a couple of coasters which took a few shots at me. I was not unrelieved when, during the afternoon, the squadron was released for the rest of the day.

I was now pretty well set in the routine of a fighter pilot's life on an established station within fairly easy reach of London. Now that most of the bomb damage had been cleared up a bit, Biggin was quite comfortable; life in the mess was pleasant and there was always company. We got forty-eight hours' leave fairly regularly and on these occasions and when the squadron was released for weather or other reasons, we used to go off to London in twos and threes and do the rounds of favourite restaurants and clubs. Sometimes there were terrific parties when most people got a bit steamed up and it was good to get rid of a lot of superfluous energy, even though we had a hangover afterwards. And we usually did!

Operations seemed to come in rushes. Either we were doing no ops and only testing our aircraft or our cannons, or practising dog-fighting and attacks; or we had plenty of operational flying. And I remember that there was fairly general agreement that the 109 pilots knew the score pretty well; too well, for we had a good many losses. By October I had been with the squadron longer than any of the other pilots with the exception of Don Kingaby. But that is getting ahead a bit.

"Mungo Park is missing," Hunk told me one day.

The CO of 74 Squadron, with his No. 2, were reported to have dived away into France from the St Omer area chasing some 109's. They were never seen or heard of again; 74 lost an experienced Battle of Britain pilot and a very popular commander.

August, 1941, was to be a busy month. But for us it started with Wimpy Wade's wedding. He and Josephine were married at Oxted, all the boys went along and the reception was at . . . yes, the "White Hart". After we had toasted Wimpy and Josephine liberally with champagne and had seen them well and truly off, there was another party which started at East Grinstead and ended at 3 a.m.!

Looking back to those August days, it seems that every time we went up there were bags of Jerries about.

The controllers became almost monotonous:

"Twenty plus Lille, angels three zero."

"Fifty plus bandits St Omer, angels two zero."

The controller had to give up once.

About 300 of our fighters were airborne; some went in ahead of the bombers on "delousing" sweeps; others were in the main "beehive" with the Blenheims and Stirlings; and others were covering the withdrawal.

The Germans put up so many 109's to saturate the area in small sections that eventually we heard the controller saying:

"Many 109's covering Northern France at all heights."

He left it to us; and we certainly felt we were being watched.

On one sweep over St Omer—the 109 lair—we really got mixed up with them.

Immediately we crossed the coast at Boulogne we were engaged. The squadron split up like a bomb burst. I soon had two 109's on my tail when I was down to 2,000 feet after taking evasive action. One began an attack, and I turned left into him. We both did a circle, and when he was opposite me on the other side of the circle, I did a hard right turn, got my sights on him and gave him a burst. At that moment his No. 2 opened up on me, and I saw tracer going over my head, a little too close for comfort. I had to break away. Suddenly I saw another 109 about fifty yards on my right; and it was my turn to fire again. He went on his back and did a slow spin into some clouds; as they were only some eighty feet above the sea I was quite satisfied that he could not have got out of that spin and that he must have gone straight into the sea.

Now it was the turn of his friends again. Two of them began to get unfriendly, so I dropped into cloud hoping they would sheer off. I dodged about in the cloud for a time; but when I put out my nose again—there they were! We began a party, and I remember that at one moment of it, as I pulled out of a dive in trying to shake them off, I blacked out partially. This was due to the aircraft tightening up in the pull-out. I was leaning forward and looking behind and I was forced on to the stick. I came-to as the Spit came out of the dive, and found that I was climbing upside down. For a moment I could not tell the difference between blue sea and blue sky. The 109's chased me to within two or three miles of Dover, and I have never given the white cliffs a bigger welcome.

My claim for an Me-109 was credited to me; and the first can of beer tasted pretty good.

1.,

A long way to go—sprog Pilot Officer, Biggin Hill, 1941.

2.,

Ready for Ops! 92 Squadron 1941.

3.,

Spitfire Vb, RAF Biggin Hill, summer, 1941.

4.,

My CO in the desert; Sqn Ldr F V Morrello, 112 Squadron.

Interesting moments did not come only in the company of Jerries. During one flight the undercarriage of my Spitfire would not lock up. Then, when I got it up, it would not come down. I had a lot of chatter over the r/t with the control tower, and got a good deal of cheerful advice from all and sundry on what I should do to get it down. In the end, after throwing the Spit about, the wheels came down all right. The day ended with my going on a show which was a diversion to a raid. We saw no Jerries, but there was foul oxygen in my bottles and I came back just about poisoned.

I was not the only pilot to report being attacked by a Spitfire. During August one of our pilots went missing; he broke formation near the English coast and was not seen again. We thought it suspicious; and we became more suspicious a few days later. A Spitfire with camouflage that we had been using a week earlier—ours had since been changed—joined up with the Biggin wing while we were returning from a sweep. A section was detailed to look him over, but he sheered off. The following day I had trouble starting my aircraft and missed getting airborne with the squadron. I took off after it, could not find it, climbed to 20,000 feet on my own and saw a lone Spitfire patrolling.

"Perhaps the Jerries have got one of our Spits and are doing a little roaming around and checking up," Hunk Humphreys said to me when I mentioned seeing this aircraft.

Several of us began to have the same feeling.

Some of the pilots in 92 were picked off about this time, 609 lost two. Another pilot from 609 went in the sea and I saw him quite by chance. We were on a show when one of 92's pilots developed engine trouble and I was detailed to escort him back to England. I left him at the English coast, turned back, stooged around and saw a dinghy. I circled, fired a red Very or two, and eventually a Lysander arrived escorting a launch. My flight lasted two-and-a-quarter hours.

A few days later I was to be grateful for Jamie Rankin's skill. I was with him and Phil Archer when the three of us were jumped by about thirty 109's. Jamie seemed to anticipate their every move, and gave us breaks into them just at the right time. It was warm work; Archer got shot up badly and was wounded in the leg, and I got a couple of bullets in the wing and a punctured tyre. We all got chased to within five miles of the English coast and went in to land at Manston short of fuel and ammunition; I was not too pleased having to touch down with a busted tyre.

The 109's were active that day, for several other Spitfires came into Manston while we were there, some badly shot up. Squadron Leader Robinson, of 609, landed with his wheels up, and one of his pilots crashed on the aerodrome, badly wounded.

There was another show that afternoon, and 92 could muster only six aircraft. Three were written off when a Sergeant collided with two others on take-off; the Sergeant died later in hospital. Gordon Brettell crash-landed near Detling, out of petrol. The day's score was: four Spitfires lost, two pilots killed, one wounded. Some day!

"Squadron's released," Gordon said and smacked me on the back a couple of days later. "Let's go up to town. I know a couple of girls at the Windmill."

It was good to forget about recent happenings. We met two of his friends, dined well, drank, and even managed to dance.

As a variation from sweeps there was always the odd "Rhubarb"—in case life became monotonous—and once I got a great kick from seeing French people waving while a couple of us flew around near Le Touquet after shooting up a factory there. I saw piles of dust and tiles burst up in clouds; and loosed off a few rounds at a tower which had a gun tripod and some sandbags on top.

We often had trouble with our 20 mm cannons. They did not always work as they should in those days, and they once made me very irritable during a sweep on St Omer. We were jumped by some 109's—the very mention of 109's eventually seemed to make the hair on the back of my neck crinkle!—and I managed to get one nicely lined up. But my cannons would not fire.

Sweeps, dawn patrols, Rhubarbs—all were routine for most of the fighter squadrons round about this period; and those of us who did not buy it began to get a bit of promotion. Towards the end of August I was made section leader of B Flight, which meant leading the flight and, on occasions, the squadron.

One patrol I led over a convoy was notable for a couple of incidents; we were vectored on to a 109 and I was able to claim a "damaged"; and my No. 2 a sergeant, got separated from us, lost himself and baled out over Eastbourne. This was regarded as a pretty bad show, particularly as he had thrown away a valuable aircraft; subsequently a court of inquiry was held.

With September there came a change at Biggin. Sailor has finished

his tour and is being posted. Jamie is the new Wingco, and Dicky Milne
has got 92.

This was the news that we heard as we lolled in our chairs at
dispersal. Our feelings were a bit mixed. We all had tremendous
admiration for Sailor, as a man and as a fighter pilot. At the same time,
92 was glad that Jamie was getting his job for he knew the score, looked
after his pilots, and had collected some Jerries pretty quickly. Dicky
Milne had arrived as a flight commander, replacing Brian Kingcome,
who had gone on rest; and though he had been with the squadron for a
short time, everybody was pleased Dicky was taking it over.

Somehow these changes made me feel a little older. The Biggin I
knew when I arrived first in April now seemed a different place; there
was a new régime, many new faces, and some of the old ones were not
coming back—ever.

The beer's on me," said Dicky Milne. And we had a terrific party.
Squadron parties were usually entirely spontaneous; little excuse was
needed, and they would begin in the ante-room or the bar quite quietly.
After an hour or so a move would be made, more likely than not to the
"White Hart" where we stayed until closing time. Then there would be a
rapid return to the mess and the party really got going until the small hours,
livened with various games such as mess rugby and hi-cockolorum.

We settled down to the new régime, and I had a pleasant spell of ten
days' leave.

"We're off to Gravesend," Dicky Milne told me when I got back.

"What, leaving Biggin?"

"Yes. We're to operate from there and link up with the Biggin wing
for any big show."

It was a wrench leaving Biggin, and none of us was quite sure
whether we would like Gravesend. It was further away from London for
one thing; but still, it was a change, and we settled in rather more
cheerfully when we found that our dispersal was a club house, and that
we could scramble straight from the bar! We were billeted at Cobham
Hall, the estate of Lord Darnley, a splendid mansion with long, ramb-
ling corridors and, of course, the reputation of having a ghost. Butch,
the squadron's bull terrier mascot, seemed to think so too, for we often
watched him standing stock-still, growling.

"Poltergeists," Hunk, who usually took charge of Butch suggested.
"Go, fetch 'em, Butch!"

Butch was content to stand and growl.

We tested out the local pubs in Gravesend, and before long began to lose our chief regrets for Biggin. I remember one spot was "Daniel's Den"; and whether it was the result of a visit to the Den, or whether it was that I began to feel I was forming bad habits, I do remember deciding to go on the waggon for a week.

Tommy Lund agreed that it might be a good thing.

"Drink and slow Spits—avoid them, my boy!" he confided.

Poor old Tommy. Two days later he went missing with a couple of others. Tony Bruce, tall, wiry, who had picked up a trick in Canada of snaring people and things with his lariat, crash-landed near Ashford. The whole of his section had been destroyed and, although we didn't know it at the time, this was the first encounter with the new FW 190 which was to do much damage. On our next escort we lost two more sergeants. The wing went in with nine Blenheims which bombed power stations and the docks at Ostend. 92 was the last squadron out, and we were met by over twenty 109's and Focke-Wulf 190's. Eight of them attacked my section; Sergeant Cox went down with flames flashing from behind his cockpit and from under his belly. We had lost five pilots in two days on comparatively easy operations. The FW 190 had arrived.

This turned out to be one of the last shows I did with 92 squadron in England. One month later—to the very day—I was taking off for Cairo!

But before that there was a tailing off of operations by 92, a lot of practice flying for new types; and somehow or other a smell of squad drill began to creep in.

"92's not what it was," Don Kingaby remarked to me one day. I can see now that it was just one of those periods that most squadrons experienced. At times a squadron would be right at the top of its form; bags of spirit, lots of flying, and good fun. Then there might be losses and changes, and something of the life of a squadron would change and fade, to come back again later.

"We're off to Digby."

That was the next news.

"Bags of red tape and bull." And that was the general comment on the place. We did not like it; we did not care for practice flying or firing at drogues. It was too far away from war, we felt. We got bored. There was some heavy drinking at times; and I even began to build a model Spitfire.

One day at the end of September, while I was at lunch in the mess, Sammy Sanderson, one of the flight commanders, marched in.

"You're either going overseas, or you're going to join the Merchant Navy and be shot off over the briny in a catapult-kite," he grinned.

I gulped.

It seemed that two pilots with my length of experience were wanted, and it was between Hunk and Phil Archer and myself to make up our minds as to who should go. Phil was very keen to join the Merchant Service Fighter Unit equipped with Hurricanes and see the world. I tossed up with Hunk for who should go to Cairo.

"Heads," I called as Hunk spun.

"Tails!"

I thought it would be a lonely trip; but that evening a signal came through ordering both Hunk and myself to Cairo—as flight commanders! We were to fly out. We got down to a heavy session at the bar.

I felt quite pleased and a little excited at the thought of going abroad. At the same time, I was sorry to be leaving 92, though the idea of staying at Digby with the squadron on rest was not a very interesting proposition. The idea was that we were to be away for six weeks; but I was soon to learn that this was the usual yarn spun to those posted to the Middle East. My six weeks turned out to be three years.

The next few days rushed by. There were my parents to telephone, tropical kit to be collected, including a splendid Kitchener-type pith helmet, and tight, drainpipe tropical trousers; a few letters to write. There was a brief trip to London to be fitted out, a visit to my people, and a tour of our favourite drinking spots—somehow I managed to knock a tooth out at the last one! Then we tore back to Digby only to learn that we were to go back to London that same night.

On November 3rd, Hunk and I with fourteen other types bound for the Middle East, got into launches at Mount Batten, Plymouth, to be ferried out to a Sunderland. It was late at night and there was a brilliant moon.

"That's Plymouth," said Hunk over my shoulder, a short time later.

As the Sunderland circled, we could see the city clearly in the soft yellow light; well blacked-out, lapped by a sheet of twinkling silver; and overhead, a star-stippled sky. Though we said nothing to one another, I suppose Hunk and I were both thinking the same thing: "When shall we see old England again?"

Many of the sixteen on board that night were never to see it again;

some were shot down into the desert; others were taken prisoner. I thought of my father and mother, and of my sister, Peg; I thought of girl friends; and of types in 92.

Soon we were well out over the sea, flying in brilliant moonlight. I was too restless, and probably still too excited, to settle down. As we got near the Portuguese coast I offered to relieve the gunner of one of the midships gun positions; I had picked up a smattering of the Vickers K gun at FTS.

"Lisbon," Hunk shouted at me later.

We could see it well enough, lights blazing for miles, none of the black-out we had left behind in England.

"Wouldn't mind a night out there!"

But Gibraltar was to be our first stop. My memories are of a bath and breakfast at the Rock Hotel; car drivers, forbidden to sound their horns, banging their hands on the outside of their car doors to clear a way; the *Ark Royal*, soon to be sunk, and a Middy who obligingly showed us over; a merchant ship with a Hurricane on its catapult; a visit to the Capitol with a warm glow on; and lights, lights everywhere.

Then on to Malta—a moonlight landing; bomb damage and desolation; the Calafrana mess and a walk, feeling warm and sticky, out to Halfar airfield; 249 scrambling after some Savoias and Macchis; Valetta and bombed ships. Then on to Feyum airfield, just outside Cairo, in a Wellington, and a very bumpy trip it was.

Into Cairo—shopping; a new tooth to replace the one I lost in London; and so by train to RAF Headquarters, Western Desert, at Maarten Bagush; our first sight of the desert, flat, brown, unattractive; and all sixteen of us, in our best blues, getting dusty and sandy; finally a small tent shared with Hunk. How far away seemed the comfortable Biggin mess!

The AOC, Air Vice-Marshal Coningham, who commanded the Western Desert Air Force which became famous and retained its title of Desert Air Force to the end of the war, gave us a talk next morning and news about a big push to Tripoli, just about to begin. Hunk and I were to join 112 Squadron, flying Curtiss P40 Tomahawks; the two other Curtiss squadrons in the wing were 250 and 3 RAAF. The plan was that the wing would move up to Tripoli, covering eighty miles a day, and then withdraw. Its job was to knock down about thirty 109's that were backing up Rommel, and to destroy any bombers attacking the army.

That evening a car arrived to take us to 112 Squadron at Sidi Hannish. The driver, a pilot, was horribly tight, and my first impressions were not very happy. He kept muttering away about minefields, and how easy it was to get lost in the desert. We were too tired to worry much, and for myself, I had a feeling of something like anti-climax after all the excitement of leaving Digby and London and England. We had, I suppose, been dumped down pretty quickly in the desert and we needed a little time to get our knees brown.

Hunk and I had a look at our camp beds in a tent on the sand.

"Not much like Biggin," he grinned. "Come on, let's find the bar."

There we soon got among 112 and found them to be good types. We met the CO, Squadron Leader Tony Morrello, Jerry Westenra, a New Zealander, one of the flight commanders, quiet, capable, for whom I soon developed a high regard; three Australians—Jack Bartle, Butch Jefferies, and Ken Sands—three of many Australians in the Western Desert, first-rate fighter pilots.

We had a look round the mess: an EPIP—"Egyptian pattern Indian patent"—tent, with coconut matting over the desert floor, several baretop, collapsible wooden tables and benches for messing; a small wooden bar, stocked with Egyptian Stella beer and American tinned beer; a few treasured and battered armchairs; the inevitable gramophone with the equally inevitable few records; and an elderly radio.

We went out and had another look at the desert—so very still and silent, with a sense of free and open space; so utterly different from the green fields of Kent; and very cold.

I shivered, and found myself thinking of 109's. Well, I been lucky so far, even managing to bag a couple and damage one or two. I wondered if my experience would be sufficient out here—120 operational hours in Spitfires.

Hunk may have been thinking along the same lines.

"Tomahawks," he said. "Tomahawks. Know anything about them?"

"Not a clue!"

I was soon to find out.

## CHAPTER 5

# *War in the Desert*

---

I PRANGED a Tomahawk on my first flight.

On the day after joining 112 Squadron on November 13th—thirteen always seemed an unlucky number with me —I crashed and I felt terrible.

Before I went up on a fifteen minute "look-see", I sat in the big, American cockpit which seemed enormous, talking with other pilots and getting the value of their experience in these aircraft, and going over all the knobs and buttons. The aircraft seemed big and heavy and it certainly packed a powerful punch with two .5 inch machine-guns on the top of the fuselage and four .3 inch machine-guns in the wings. These guns were cocked by levers, the breeches of the .5's protruded into the cockpit and, I was to discover later, gave off clouds of exciting smelling cordite when they were fired.

I took off quite normally but my first impressions were not very encouraging after being used to Spitfires. The performance of the Tomahawk seemed poor and its rate of climb was slow; but still it was fun to be flying again and to get a view of the desert from another angle. When I came in to land I did the normal three-point Spitfire landing, ground looped and ended in a heap. The next thing I knew was that I had broken off both undercarriage legs and the Tomahawk was sliding sideways into the sand, raising great clouds of dust, and both wheels were shooting off through the air of their own accord.

It was a far worse sensation than going over on the nose of the Spitfire I at Grangemouth for then I had been a pupil and not even in a squadron. But here I was, supposed to be operationally experienced, a new boy to a squadron, breaking up one of their aircraft at a time when every machine was precious.

"Cheer up." said Hunk, "It might have happened to anyone."

But I had been the one, and I remember, when all the fuss was over, strolling off by myself, looking out over the sand, hating it and feeling homesick and having a crazy feeling of wanting to run out into the desert away from everything. Later on, chatting to Hunk in the bar, I tried to console myself by saying:

"Oh well, it's only for six weeks. Then we'll be back in England."

There was some rather mocking laughter from one or two people who overheard this remark—how well they knew that one about going home in six weeks—and I began to feel rather bitter. But this fit of depression soon passed.

The following morning I took up a Tomahawk again, flew around for an hour, and put it down all right, mastering the necessary "wheel landing" technique. And there was plenty to keep our minds occupied when the squadron moved up to a forward base known as 110 Airfield, south of Sidi Barrani.

It took me some time, however, to get used to conditions in the desert, for which I had no great liking at first, both on the ground and in the air. Once Hunk and I got lost coming back after a flight over Sidi Barrani and Mersa Matruh but somehow managed to scramble home; and, on another occasion while returning after patrolling over British tanks, a terrific sandstorm blew up. Within moments visibility was reduced to a couple of hundred yards and there was sand everywhere—in the eyes, nose, ears and mouth and, almost it seemed, in the brain. Sand got inside our clothes and into our food; everything seemed to feel and to taste of grit. How far away seemed good old Biggin.

"The flap's on," Hunk announced one morning.

The tanks we had patrolled above were moving forward for the Auchinleck-Rommel battles, the offensive which was planned to end in Tripoli but got stuck at El Agheila and then turned into a retreat as Rommel panzered the British forces back again.

Our wing was to patrol over the Tobruk-Gambut area and for the second time in four days we moved up, this time to 122 Airfield near Fort Madellena on the Egypt-Libya border which was defined by mile after mile of barbed wire, running from the coast at Sollum deep into the desert.

When we arrived at 122 Airfield we found that we had no beds so Hunk and I settled down together on the sand, back to back for extra warmth. We were to get quite used to this sort of thing both in advance and retreat, and we usually slept fully clothed on the bare sand, covering ourselves with blankets and flying kit. During a battle period it was quite normal not to shave or to wash for days on end, partly due to the shortage of water.

Tobruk was now being relieved and while some terrific tank battles were being fought we patrolled in sixes, eights, or twelves either over the battle area or escorting Blenheims bombing enemy troop positions.

During our first sortie we ran into six Me-110's and there was such a mix-up that I seemed to spend most of my time dodging Tomahawks. We also met up with some Italian fighters, two Fiat CR 42's, very manoeuvrable biplanes. I shared one of them with two other pilots of 112 but it was not a very satisfactory fight.

The Italian did a couple of turns, went down to land, nosed over with the aircraft going on its back. The pilot was out in a flash, bolting away from the Fiat like a scared rabbit. The two other Tomahawks began chasing him and shooting him up, but I had no stomach for this sort of thing and concentrated on setting fire to his machine. While making my run-in to pepper the Fiat I flew low over him as he ran, completely terrified, stumbling in his flying kit. After I had hit the Fiat I turned and looked out for him. He was dead, spread-eagled on the ground and our own troops were coming up to collect him. Somehow this rather shocked me for although I was fully aware during a fight that it was either my life or the other chap's, yet it always seemed to me that I was fighting a machine and not another pilot. I felt that way to the end of the war.

There was a more businesslike mix-up the next day when, a mixed formation of Hurricanes and Tomahawks led by the wing leader, Wing Commander Jefferies, an Australian, we ran into several 109 F's. Sergeant Tom Burney was shot down and belly-landed and Wing Commander Fred Rozier went down with his Hurricane to pick him up. Rozier was a Battle of Britain pilot, extremely popular and with a fine record. He was later to become a group captain and to do great work for the Desert Air Force. He got his Hurricane down all right and picked up Burney, but while the machine was taking off a tyre burst. They sorted themselves out of the crash and walked back to the airstrip from well behind the enemy lines.

While this was going on I got mixed up with a 109 and was horrified when my gunsight failed. There was only one thing to do—use the fixed ring and bead sight. I was rather surprised by the result. One of the

Australians, Bobbie Gibbs, described it later by saying, "The bastard just flew to pieces". The pilot baled out and while he floated gently down with his parachute swinging from side to side I circled round him and waved, a rather silly thing to do for I would have been easy meat for any of his friends. He waved back to me but once he touched the ground he bolted off for a bush and flung himself down flat. He was quite safe as far as I was concerned and he was later taken prisoner. I still have his photo in my log book.

Our fighters were not having it all their own way by any means and in only four sorties we lost fourteen Tomahawks, most of them shot down by 109's. Occasionally we came across Italians in the Macchi 200 and Fiat G50, slippery customers and very manoeuvrable.

It was not long before I was shot down myself and posted missing twice in five days.

The first time was on Sunday, November 30th.

"There's to be a dawn wing patrol over the El Gobi area. Twelve from 112, twelve from the Aussies," Hunk told me adding, "Bags of activity."

We went off in boxes of four, climbed to 10,000 feet on course for the battle area. Some chattering began on the r/t and then about 2,000 feet below and ahead of us I saw a gaggle of thirty to forty aircraft, German and Italian, a mixture of Junkers 87 and escorting 109's, Macchis and Fiats. Soon the wing was peeling off, going right into them.

I found a G50 in front of me. He dived for the deck and seemed determined to get away for he just streaked a few feet over the desert taking no evasive action except for an occasional violent switch-back motion. I stayed with him, finding him extremely hard to hit and using up considerable ammunition until he crash-landed. That was that.

But some of his friends had watched the chase and followed it too, and now they had me all to themselves. There were about three or four 109 F's and the odd G50. I forget how many of their attacks I dodged, probably four or five, but I managed to get a few shots at a 109 F and saw him start to spurt glycol.

Now it was my turn to run and I bolted for home, right down on the deck and flat out, with the Allison pulling its full boost of 50 inches. I knew that there was at least one 109 F after me and I knew he could move faster. And, unlike me, he was not short of ammunition. I soon found that he was no ordinary pilot and a very good shot as well. I wondered later whether it was the German ace Marseille.

Bullets began to smack into my wings and into the rear fuselage. I did a violent vertical left-hand turn a few hundred feet or so above the ground, but with a good shot from fully 90 degrees of deflection the Jerry hit my left wing and I heard the tremendous bang of an explosive shell.

I am still not quite clear what happened after that. I remember the Tomahawk turning on its back and seeing the ground far too few feet below—or rather above!—the cockpit. I know that I saw the sand come rushing up and that I kicked the rudder and pushed the stick over and back entirely by instinct.

There was a whirl of sky and desert. And then the world came right way up and I could feel that I had control of the Tomahawk again. It hit the sand with its belly and bounced. Up we went, and down again, down in a crash-landing. And now it was my turn to get out and bolt.

I scrambled out of the cockpit and found myself closing the cockpit hood with a subconscious action, hoping that the Jerry would think I was still in it and not look for me behind a bush. I ducked under the engine, looking anxiously round for some bushes; the Tomahawk was on fire and I remember thinking that it had probably been on fire while we were in the air together. The 109 was swinging round obviously preparing to shoot me up. I saw some scrub about twenty yards away, covered that distance in a record time, flung myself down flat behind it, and wished that it had grown higher than one foot.

The 109 F arrived with a snarl and I heard the horrible crack and whistle and whine of bullets. I cringed into the sand, expecting to be hit. I heard cannon-shells exploding as they banged into the Tomahawk and then the 109 F droning away. And then the silence of the desert, broken only by the crackling of flames licking the Tomahawk, now a black wreck against a clear blue sky. I watched the 109. Was he coming back? I continued to lie flat and still, listening to the flames, hoping the sound would not be over-toned by the Messerschmitt returning. But he never came back.

I sat there by the scrub for some time, getting over my fright, wondering what to do next, watching my aircraft going up in smoke and listening to the rattle of the last few rounds of my ammunition exploding. For a time I felt almost mesmerized, for it seemed uncanny to find myself squatting there in the middle of the desert. One moment I had been in the centre of noise with the desert coming towards me far too quickly. Now everything was silent and static and the desert seemed a very big and a very lonely place.

I soon decided that I could not continue to sit there long. The Tomahawk was sending up a thick column of black smoke, and the wrong people might become curious. I made a quick check-up; I had my revolver and water-bottle, my escape compass built into a uniform button, and a good pair of desert boots. I unscrewed the compass from the button, and with a vague idea that I must be somewhere south of El Adem and on the wrong side of the enemy lines, I checked an easterly course with the sun. There was only one thing to do. I began walking.

I felt hot, slightly dazed and very thirsty as I plodded on for about half an hour over the sand. I found a track and began to follow it, keeping a crafty eye out on the horizon from time to time. I was not altogether surprised when, a little while later, I sighted a lorry. It seemed to be travelling quite fast, bouncing along towards the cloud of black smoke which was the funeral pyre of my aircraft.

One of ours or a Jerry?

I found some scrub and rock and scuttled behind it as the lorry came along the track, approaching me. The drone of its motor grew louder; now it was going past. I took a quick peep. One of ours!

I stood up quickly.

"Hi! Wait a minute."

The lorry pulled up in a few yards and out jumped four or five figures gripping rifles and revolvers. For an awful moment I thought I had made a mistake and that they were Jerries; by their clothes they might have been anybody.

However, they were Desert Rats, in quite irregular uniform, and they seemed, after a couple of seconds, to have no doubt that I was RAF.

"My name's Duke," I said, "112 Squadron and"—pointing to the smoke—"that is, or was, my aircraft."

"So you got out of it all right," one of them said. "We saw you from quite a distance away, upside down with a Jerry beating you up. Never thought you'd walk away from that one."

I had a wonderful feeling of relief to be talking with them, among friends, no longer lonely, on my own. When one of them produced a hip flask with what appeared to be sleight of hand and gave me a good nip of whisky, and another lit and handed me a cigarette I felt they were the best chaps in the world.

While we were chatting and I was telling them what had happened, we heard the drone of an aircraft. We all took a quick look.

"It's a Lysander."

It was a Lysander all right, following the desert track, making towards the pillar of smoke.

"Let's give him a wave," I suggested. "If he sees us and can get down, maybe I can thumb a ride home."

We all began shouting and waving. The aircraft circled but the pilot seemed to be hesitating about landing. Then he straightened up and began to come down, landing a short distance away from the lorry.

Out got the pilot—and a general. Now we realized why there had been a slight hesitation about landing. The general was looking for Advanced Army Headquarters and was not having much joy in the confusion of a rapid advance. We pored over Army maps, and decided that we were in an area of no-man's land.

"We'd better be off before Rommel has a shufti at that smoke himself," said the pilot. "Hop in, Duke."

I said a quick good-bye to my Desert Rat friends, squeezed into the back of the Lysander with the general, and was thoroughly happy to be flying over the desert again—it's so much quicker than walking. Eventually, we found Advanced Army Headquarters and, after the general had completed his talk, off we went again.

"We'll drop you at your airfield," said the general.

When we landed I thanked them and watched the Lysander take-off again. I liked that aircraft!

It was now evening—Sunday evening—and years seemed to have passed since I had taken off that morning with the squadron. I walked slowly over the soft sand to the camp, glad to be home again. As I approached the mess I noticed a small group of pilots and the padre. He was holding a church service and suddenly I felt intensely moved. Here we were in a lonely spot of the desert, yet here was home and a church service at the end of an all too eventful day.

As I continued walking slowly towards the small group, almost instinctively starting to move on tiptoe so that I should not disturb them, a few heads turned and there was some quick, quiet whispering. I did not know it then, but I had been posted missing—a signal eventually reaching my father and mother at Tonbridge.

I had never seen old Hunk Humphreys praying before, and when he looked up suddenly and saw me the pleasure that lighted his face somehow startled, and then surprised and delighted me. I went down on my knees and joined in silent prayer. I had much to be grateful for.

That night I slept restlessly. I kept on waking up, seeing the sandy desert rushing towards me; but fortunately we had a quiet spell for a day or two and I found I was quite all right while I was flying.

"Don't you go doing a thing like that again," Hunk said.

I replied that I had no such intention; but the following Thursday was quite exciting.

Ten aircraft from 112 and twelve from 250 met up with another collection of Junkers, 109's, Macchi's and G50's. This time I managed to break up a bunch of Junkers 87's in close formation by spraying them with machine-gun fire. I saw one begin a gentle dive, smoking a bit; but when a 109 began nosing after me I decided to leave the Junkers alone.

Then a Macchi 200 appeared to think that I was his meat and we had quite a good dog-fight before he began to beetle off home. The Italian pilot seemed a cheerful type and once did a complete roll in front of me while I chased him. I was not altogether amused because my guns developed some kind of trouble and stopped working one by one until I had only a cannon firing, and eventually I had to cock that every time before tiring. Finally it packed up too, and to keep up the chase I had to make a number of vigorous and threatening dummy attacks on the Macchi.

All this time we had been flying a few feet above the sand and once we chased out over the sea. Suddenly I saw Tobruk come ripping up below and a number of soldiers waving. The Italian was a bit put off by one of my dummy attacks; he went into a steep turn, stalled, flicked over the other way and went straight into the ground to explode with a burst of flame.

I landed on Tobruk aerodrome to re-fuel and get my guns fixed up, and enjoyed some lunch of bully beef and biscuit with the Aussie Army. I was as surprised as they to find myself back again at Tobruk the following day.

It began with our wing meeting up with another circus and shooting down ten Jerries. I was leading a section of four and not feeling particularly happy. On take-off clouds of sand raised by the leading section resulted in my perspex canopy becoming thickly coated with dust, restricting my vision. Then my radio packed up and I felt very lonely, not being able to hear what was going on; but as our numbers were few and there was a hope of meeting the enemy circus I decided against leaving the formation and going home.

The sun was brilliant, almost blinding when I glanced towards it occasionally, knowing it was from that direction we could expect trouble from 109's; and the combination of the sanded canopy and the glare of the sun had me blinking and peering. I felt a little blind, and, without the radio, quite deaf. I hung on to the formation and soon I saw our leader breaking down into a gaggle of Junkers 87 and a close escort of Macchi's and Fiat G 50's.

Down we went but there was to be no joy for me. There was a top cover of 109's all right but with my sanded-up canopy and the sun I had missed them. One of them did not miss me. There was an abrupt bang in the cockpit on the starboard side. My foot was knocked off the rudder peddle, I felt a violent blow on my right leg and the cockpit filled with smoke. The banging continued, making the Tomahawk shudder, and I took some pretty quick evasive action, knowing that the aircraft had been badly hit.

At 10,000 feet the Tomahawk went into a spin: its right elevator was completely shot away, the right wing torn at the trailing edge by cannon shell, and the right aileron control shot through. Though I did my best to straighten out, the aircraft spun—and spun. Time to get out, I thought. I undid my safety straps, opened the hood and got ready to leave; and then, at about 2,000 feet, the machine began to behave itself again. It straightened out.

I had no intention of taking another walk in the desert if it could be avoided, and decided to make off for Tobruk, keeping an anxious and wary eye on a 109 high above. With a damaged wing and only one aileron and fifty per cent the elevators, I reckoned on an eventful landing for I was unable to control the aircraft at a speed below one hundred and fifty miles per hour; and now my safety straps were undone.

The Tomahawk touched down at one hundred and fifty and I began a bumpy ride, rattling around in the cockpit, trying to hold on to the aircraft with one hand and protect myself with the other. When the machine stopped I was out very smartly in case it should catch fire; it didn't, but it was a complete write-off and so I collected its clock as a souvenir, which I still have with me at Dunsfold.

"Strewth," said an Australian voice. "It's Duke back again. This joker must like this place. Thought you were low flying until you hit the deck."

I had little appetite for bully beef at that second lunch in Tobruk; and while I was having my leg attended to at the emergency hospital the Jerries provided their daily blitz with artillery and Stukas. This seemed a bit excessive in Tobruk's confined space and I was not at all sorry when I was offered a lift back to 122 Airfield in a Blenheim. We took off in the evening, streaked out over the sea at nought feet, and returned to the squadron to find I had been posted missing again—without my radio I had been unable to report what had been happening. I hobbled around, feeling quite a little bit proud of my "wound", and during sympathetic conversations occasionally picking out bits of cannon shell splinters to prove its authenticity.

I reported my return to our commanding officer, Squadron Leader Morrello. He smiled at me and said:

"Making a bit of a habit of this sort of thing, aren't you? What about nipping down to Cairo for a short spell of leave?"

I thanked him, flew a Tomahawk that required repairing to Feyum, and spent five wonderful days in Cairo, beginning with a full hour spent soaking in a hot bath followed by a tremendous meal and some steady drinking. It must have been a good leave for I had no money for dinner on my last night, or even for breakfast the following morning. I enjoyed the rest and the change but I found that Cairo soon palled after a few days. I was glad to return to the squadron.

It had moved forward to El Adem and I flew a Tomahawk for three and a quarter hours before catching up with it. Rommel was now on the run and we had further moves, on to Gazala and to Mechili. Everywhere was the wreckage of battle and at Mechili many dead bodies were still lying around. We looted the fort and some Italian lorries, risking booby traps to make ourselves more comfortable. Winter was setting in, the desert looked even more bare and barren, and there were times when, chatting among ourselves, in the bar, we pondered whether there was any strategic value to North Africa or in winning the desert. We knew there was.

Fortunately there was little time for introspection. The wing was kept busy and during one sweep I was able to get some of my own back. We were flying in loose fours at 4,000 feet top cover when I saw some Junkers 87 in vics of three circling Megrun airfield and dived on them, followed by Sergeant Carson, my No. 2. We were both certain that we had hit a Junkers and were shooting up some others when I saw a 109 F taking-off. After a long chase towards the sea, it seemed that the Messerschmitt crashed near the coast; and as I was now alone I climbed for cloud and began to make for Mechili. While over the coast south of Benghazi I spotted a neat formation of Junkers 52 heading for Benina and felt that my luck was too good to be true. I picked on a straggler with a few quick bursts, but after it began to go down I became rather too busy to see what happened for some 110's dropped down out of cloud. With little ammunition left I was not too keen on a party, went up into cloud myself and reported Junkers to wing operations when I got back to Mechili. They were attended to by some Hurricanes who ground strafed them.

The advance continued, the Army entered Benghazi, and the wing moved up seventy miles to Msus, where we celebrated Christmas Day. It was the first time I had been away from Tonbridge for Christmas and I prepared for it by taking time off to have a wash and brush up for the first time in three days. After dinner—bully soup, steak and bully pie, biscuits, jam, tea, and one tin of beer—we linked up with 250 Squadron, gossiping in our tents, binding a bit about lack of aircraft. It now took four squadrons to make up a wing of a dozen aircraft; 112 could muster five and 250 had only two serviceable. There was a rumour that we should be getting Kittyhawks, and it proved correct. At the end of December we went down to Suez, beat up Cairo mildly at night after a flight down in an old Bristol Bombay transport, and collected our new aircraft.

The Curtiss Kittyhawk was a great improvement on the Tomahawk. It had a more powerful Allison engine and six .5inch guns, and I enjoyed my first flight, a two hour run from Kasfareet to Mersa Matruh. The second flight, on New Year's Day, 1942 was not quite so good. Six of us had been told to push on quickly to El Adem but only one arrived. Trouble began with a patch of soft sand on the Mersa Matruh airfield; and while taxiing for take-off one sergeant pranged his machine and another got bogged down. So there were four.

We took off with sand beginning to blow up and after half an hour flew straight into a sandstorm. I decided to press on for El Adem while the other three turned back, and climbed up above the storm. Yellow

5.,

Curtiss P 40 Tomahawk of 112 Squadron. It was different from the Spitfire V we flew in England.

6.,

One of my Kittyhawk fighters in 112 Squadron. Note the variation of our Shark's mouth with the previous picture.

7.,

P 40 cockpit. Note gun-sight.

8.,

My second CO in 112 Squadron, Clive "Killer" Caldwell DSO, DFC (left), with my good friend "Hunk" Humphries.

9.,

Shortly after the award of the DFC—P 40 cockpit.

10.,

The boys of 112 Squadron, (left to right) Sqn Ldr C R Caldwell, Sgt W Carson, Sgt Taylor, Neville Duke, Sgt Drew, FO Humphreys, Sgt Burney, Sgt Donkin, Sgt Leu, FO Dickinson, Sgt K Carson.

11.,

The Me 109 pilot I shot down near
Sidi Rezegh, November, 1941.

12.,

Another Me 109 pilot I shot down—March,
1943. He has the Iron Cross second class
and was wounded in the right arm.

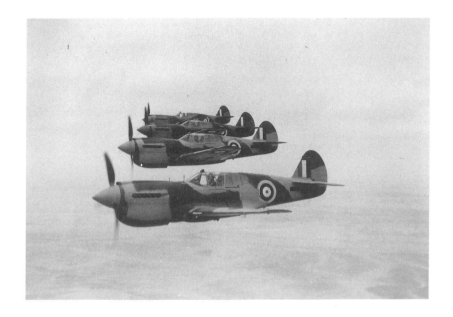

13.,

The first P 40E Kittyhawks to arrive on 112 Squadron, late 1941.

14.

Press photo—now with 92 Squadron, again, and flying Spitfires once more.

15.,

I let "my German" look over my Spitfire, QJ-S (ER336), although I shot him down in "R" (ER220).

dust blotted out the desert below and soon I lost my bearings and had to head for El Adem on a compass course. The petrol gauge began to fall and the coolant temperature to rise until it went right off the clock; and warning lights, with which the Kitty was liberally sprinkled, started to flicker. Then the windscreen oiled up and I could see nothing ahead. Fortunately, I managed to pick up Gazala, turn back for Tobruk and follow the road to El Adem, the storm still blinding. I got down all right, but the petrol tanks were just about dry.

That night I slept on the sand again and the next morning, the storm over, the others arrived. One of the sergeants who had turned back flew into a telegraph pole while landing by the desert road during the storm and was killed.

It took a week for all the Kittyhawks to reach Msus and for the squadron to become operational again. News from the front was not so good for the advance to Tripoli was held up at Agadabia, and the weather became miserable with more sandstorms, rain and cold gales. We felt cold both by day and by night. There were changes in the squadron, with the CO going on rest and Hunk Humphreys becoming a Flight Lieutenant. We celebrated his second ring with six bottles of Vat 69, and for a time the desert seemed a slightly less unfriendly place.

We did some practice flying with our new Kittyhawks, praying that they would be able to hold a 109 in a climb, for the Jerries had some unpleasant habits, which were also good tactics. They would sit upstairs in the sun, whistle down on us, and then shoot upstairs again, going up like a lift and leaving us well behind. The Kittyhawks turned out to be an improvement on the Tomahawks, but we were still outclimbed by the 109's.

Shortly after the New Year, and on my twentieth birthday, we were to escort bombers attacking Rommel's line at El Agheila. It was a Sunday. I had memories of another Sunday and perhaps this made me more than usually cautious. I was careful to do up the safety-straps properly when I got into the Kittyhawk before take-off. It was just as well that I did fasten them securely for I was no sooner airborne than smoke began to gush out from under the instrument panel. It was so thick that I could hardly see. The only thing I could do was to crash-land: close the throttle, switch off the engine, dodge some army trucks and trenches and piles of earth, and put the aircraft down with a thud.

I got out smartly, with a lump on my forehead the size of a duck egg, expecting the aircraft to go up in smoke; but it didn't, which was something of an anti-climax. It was not the best of ways to celebrate a birthday, but I was most thankful that I had done up my safety-straps, otherwise, I should have left most of my head on the instrument panel.

Rommel dug in west of El Agheila, the weather cleared and brightened with sunshine, we moved up to an airstrip at Antelat. There were celebrations for the arrival of the new CO, Squadron Leader "Killer" Caldwell, DFC and Bar, and a pep talk by Air Marshal Coningham who mentioned that two Spitfire squadrons were due to arrive shortly.

The rain returned and continued for several days; the squadrons were released but there was nowhere to go and nothing to do. The camp and the airstrip became boggy and Jerry began to send over bombers, perhaps guessing that our Kittyhawks were grounded. Rommel came out on armed reconnaisance and it was decided that the squadrons should move back to Msus. The retreat to El Alamein had begun.

There was quite a scene when we took off, for several aircraft sank quickly into the soft ground, some of them with their wing tips touching the mud; and the Army had their hands full hauling them clear. The strip runway was fairly short resulting in some hair-raising take-offs, machines just staggering into the air and waffling over the tops of lorries. The general excitement increased when a shufti-kite appeared while some twenty aircraft were congregated at one end of the runway; we hoped he was not reporting to his friends. I was the last to take-off, the sun blinded me temporarily on the run down the strip, causing me to swing to one side, and churn through a pile of shovels which went flying away merrily left and right. But the Kittyhawk flew on.

At Msus we learned that Rommel had broken out of E1 Agheila with a flying armoured column of 2,000 vehicles, including tanks. On dawn patrol the following morning we flew over a pocket of Germans near our old airstrip at Antelat; they had no shortage of Bredas and other light flak. Apparently we had left the airfield only an hour or two before they arrived. Returning at Msus we found that we were to move back to Mechili and there was a general atmosphere of alarm and despondency, nobody knowing anything definite about anything at all.

Two days later, while escorting Blenheims out to bomb any target they could find, we discovered the road from Agedabia to Antelat packed with the Afrika Korps; after the bombs had gone down we set about strafing lorries, and this became a main occupation for several days. It was exciting and risky, risky if you returned for a second run; for by then all the ack-ack was prepared. I soon decided that one run was quite sufficient: it seemed best to climb up-sun and dive to ground level well before reaching a convoy. Once you began firing you could see the bullets spurting up the sand; then you lifted the nose of the aircraft slightly until they were going right into the lorries; another slight lift and you were up and over the convoy, skimming low again seeking the cover of any slight dip in the ground. It was exciting, though I usually felt sorry for the Jerries at that moment, animated little figures trying to dodge the spurts of dust racing towards them, some of them falling, but the spurts continuing.

Our retreat continued, back to Gazala. At this point I was told to go right back to Sidi Barrani and to meet up there with 94 Squadron to pass on information about operating the new Kittyhawk. While on the way to Sidi Barrani by truck I spent a night-stop lying out in the desert. There was a full moon and the sky was bright with stars; a biting wind woke me in the morning and, lying there, I watched the sun rise, first streaking the horizon with crimson and then, as its tip appeared, long shadows gradually spreading from the rocks and scrub. At this moment it seemed not such a bad desert.

No. 94 Squadron was led by the celebrated "Imshi" Mason. I was later to fly on the show with him when he went missing after strafing Martuba Airfield. But at this particular moment nobody at 110 Airfield wanted me and he sent me packing to Cairo for leave.

When next I caught up with 112 it had moved back to Gambut and I was in time to fly with the wing when it shot down sixteen German and Italian aircraft without loss on Valentine's Day, February 14th. Coming out of cloud at about 9,000 feet we found a number of Macchi's and Breda's ground-strafing our troops south-west of Acroma. I led a section to attack ten Macchis, managing to hit one which spun in. A dog-fight followed and we used 109 tactics, diving from cloud cover and attacking and then making off for cloud again. An Australian and I finished off our particular show by chasing a Macchi at ground level and shooting it down into an army camp which it had recently been strafing.

This was to be one of the last useful sorties I did with 112. There were various spurts of excitement, such as the time when we were ground-strafed by 109's at Gambut while on stand-by and seven of our aircraft were pretty well destroyed, including mine.

One morning, early in March, I was told to report to the CO Squadron Leader Caldwell. When I marched into his caravan and saluted, I thought that he looked up at me rather bleakly.

"Anything on your mind, Duke?" he asked abruptly.

I thought hastily about one or two parties; it could not be anything to do with them.

"No, sir."

"Quite sure?"

"Yes, sir."

Caldwell grinned and winked at me, while he produced a DFC ribbon.

"Groupy asked me to give you this. It's an immediate award. Congratulations."

There was quite a session that night and though I faded away at half-past one in the morning the party was still going strong. I was now credited officially with eight enemy aircraft, two back in England and six out in the desert. Life quietened down for me for a time and there was another spell of leave.

After another short period with the squadron I was told that my first operational tour had ended. I had completed one hundred and sixty-one sorties and flown on operations for two hundred and twenty hours. During the middle of April, just a little more than a year after I had joined 92 at Biggin Hill, I was posted with Hunk Humphreys to the Fighter School at El Ballah on the Suez Canal. We were to become instructors for the period of our rest tour.

## CHAPTER 6

# *Cairo to Cape Bon*

WE arrived at El Ballah, north of Ismailia situated in a salt pan with very high humidity, on April 24th, 1942. Its full title was "Middle East Fighter School" and our job as instructors was to teach pupils to fly and fight with Tomahawks and Kittyhawks after a period of dual instruction on Harvards; there would be no more operational flying for us until we had completed our rest period.

The months at El Ballah seemed long and rather dreary although there was one period when, for some reason, it seemed that the so-called nervous types were directed to me for handling. The days ticked by with long hours of dual flying, dog-fighting and air combat; from time to time many accidents occurred when pupils killed themselves or wrote off their aircraft. One lost himself and crashed in the desert.

With the return of summer the heat became so intense that perspiration dripped and streamed from us even while we were sitting limply; we cursed and killed thousands of flies, and made sure of a daily swim either at Ismailia or in the Suez Canal. Hunk and I were delighted when we acquired two very old Spitfire I's from Middle East Headquarters, Heliopolis. They had belonged to the Turks and, without guns or radio, they were as light as feathers to fly; and it was the sheer pleasure of being in one that resulted in the Station Commander appointing me as Orderly Officer for seven days—he saw me doing aerobatics at a height not recognized as being safe by King's Regulations.

We also received a Messerschmitt 109 F from Middle East Headquarters, but I never flew it for I found great difficulty in getting myself into the small cockpit. The Station Commander, Wing Commander Linnard, DFC, took it up, however, and had an alarming flight when an oil pipe burst and drenched him with hot engine oil. Although his face and eyes were smothered with the stuff he got it down again on the ground in one piece, a remarkable effort.

Hunk and I were quite content with the old Spitfires, hoping that we should fly them again when we returned to operations, for a good supply was now arriving in the Middle East. Although I quite liked the Kittyhawk, I was keen to fly Spitfires in combat again. We thought our chance might have arrived when Rommel broke through to El Alamein; we both applied to join a squadron but were told firmly that our rest period of six months was not yet completed.

Rommel's advance, however, made a short change in our lives, for the school was moved to Muqueblia, near Haifa in Palestine, so that El Ballah could be used by a Baltimore wing. We stayed at Muqueblia for three weeks and enjoyed a change from the sand and the heat and the monotony of Egypt in a land that seemed to be green and golden and where the birds sang and the air smelled sweetly. We moved around Palestine as much as possible, visiting Nazareth, Haifa and Tel Aviv; and then, towards the end of July when the military situation in Egypt had improved, or at least had got no worse, back we returned to El Ballah and I am afraid that I disliked it more than ever, and I was itching to get to squadron life.

One piece of good news, however, was that 92 Squadron—"my" squadron, as I always like to think of it—had arrived in the Middle East and I began to bombard the commanding Officer, now Squadron Leader Wedgwood, DFC, with letters asking to join his squadron. He answered that he had already applied for me, but the request had been refused as I had not completed my rest tour. And so the months and the instructing dragged by and I was still at El Ballah when the Battle of El Alamein was fought in October. In November I borrowed a Tomahawk and flew off to seek 92 Squadron in the desert and to ask Wedgwood to apply for me again. I found him at Sidi Barrani; this time we were more successful. Not long after I returned to El Ballah an order came through posting me to 92 Squadron, and on November 18th I boarded a Lockheed at Almaza, landed at Gambut and found Wedgwood waiting for me there with a jeep. It was good to be back among the dust and the grins.

The tide of the war in North Africa had changed; El Alamein was by now one of the successful victories of history; Rommel was on the run again, chased by the Eighth Army and the Desert Air Force, and he was to keep on running until the Germans were chased right out of North Africa.

The Afrika Korps was in the region of Benghazi when I rejoined 92 Squadron at Sidi Barrani. I found that the ground personnel of 92 were little changed from the days at Biggin Hill and Gravesend; it was good to meet them all again and to make fresh friends—Ted Sly and Jeff Rose, two Australians; "Sweetwater" Scuddy, an American, Baker and Doc Savage, both Englishmen; Norris, an American; and "Topsy" Turvey, a Canadian. The squadron was flying Spitfire Vb's which were a bit slower than the standard Spitfire, being modified to suit the desert and fitted with a large air cleaner under the nose. This cleaner caused slight drag; but even so the Vb was a source of abiding content.

The first operation of my second tour was a defence patrol of Tobruk Harbour with Squadron Leader Wedgwood, reviving memories of earlier visits. And other memories were recalled as the advance continued and the squadron, which formed a wing with 601 and 145, moved up to Msus and began sweeps over El Agheila and Agadabia.

I soon settled back again to desert conditions and, finding the same old trouble of the cockpit canopy sanding up badly on take-off, I tried flying without a hood for a period, also removing from my machine any equipment I regarded as surplus, in order to lighten it to get a better performance against the 109's. But I found that, while visibility was excellent without the hood, the aircraft's speed was cut down by increased drag, and the slipstream in the cockpit was troublesome. It was also very cold.

It was winter once more and in the keen air of the desert we developed enormous appetites; food became more than usually important, particularly as supplies were not always as adequate as they might have been. A habit developed of a "yaffle" box being kept in every tent. In it was stored any food that we could lay hands on: gazelle meat, which tasted like venison, collected during shoots in the desert and butchered expertly by the Aussies, Ted Sly and Glendinning being particularly useful with their knives; sausages, cocoa, tinned food, flour, raisins, sugar, and biltong or salted antelope from East Africa. The Aussies and Canadians in the squadron usually had well-filled yaffle boxes, replenished regularly by food parcels from their friends and relatives.

On cold nights, when the wind had a bitter touch and sand seemed to be flying everywhere, it was one of the more pleasant things in life to gather four or five in a tent, and with the help of a petrol fire in a cut-down tin filled with sand, to contrive a hot meal. I can still see the inside of a tent, a few rather ragged looking types grouped round the petrol fire, the solemn and anxious looks on their faces picked out by the soft lighting, intent on producing yaffle. And then, when the cooking was completed, the sharing of the food, which warmed and cheered us and thawed us into general conversation until a move was made to turn in for the night. We talked of many things, usually closely associated with our lives—the trouble we were inclined to get with sand jamming our guns, battle formations and enemy tactics.

There was nothing static about our lives; the continuing advance meant frequent moves, the personnel of the squadron changed from time to time. From Msus we went on again to Antelat, the peak point of our advance earlier in the year, and then on to El Hassiat, ninety miles south-east of Agadabia. A new commanding officer took over, Squadron Leader Morgan replacing Squadron Leader Wedgwood, whose tour had expired. We were shocked to learn a week or two later that Wedgwood had been killed. He was a passenger in a Halifax with a Polish crew which crashed in Malta shortly after take-off for England.

We moved on again to Nogra, only eighteen miles from the front, and when the Afrika Korps was pushed back from El Agheila we covered the New Zealand Division while it put in the first of its famous left hooks.

We settled in at El Merduna for Christmas, rigged up a bar in the mess with the tail-plane of a 109, collected scrub for a Christmas tree, and various artists improved the tent walls with caricatures. Christmas Eve was enlivened with a scramble which meant climbing to 25,000 feet south-east of Nofilia; and when I returned, the Christmas lorry which had been reported "missing" on the way from Cairo, causing cursing and despondency, had at last arrived; and the remainder of the night was not particularly silent or holy.

On Christmas Day several of us made the rounds of 601 and 145 Squadrons before, in time-honoured custom, serving the airmen their Christmas dinner. Jerry Westenra and Jack Bartle, now on rest, arrived in a DH 86 ambulance plane, and everybody sat down to an enormous meal of turkey, pork, Christmas pudding, wine and various trimmings. The day ended with another visit to the airmen's mess and a further session on our own.

We were on the move again before the New Year was in, this time to El Chel, a big, square airfield; but the front had rolled on to Misurata and we were almost out of range once more. New Year's Eve was notable for a visit by Air Chief Marshal Tedder, who was making a farewell round being handing over to Air Chief Marshal Sholto Douglas; and also for a gazelle hunt when we bagged a couple while travelling at forty miles per hour in a jeep. Hunk Humphreys was sitting in front of me when I fired a .303 at one, and he complained of being deaf for a long time afterwards.

With El Chel being rather far behind the lines we began to use Tamet as a forward landing ground.

"109's are making a habit of providing the boys there with bombing and strafing for breakfast, so we shall have to look out," Morgan told us.

We took off at dawn in cold, biting weather but arrived over Tamet to find that Jerry had been a little early and had just completed the morning delivery—three a day were usually made during this period. We landed amid some confusion and stood by in our cockpits waiting to be scrambled for the second visit; and when we were sent up I led a section to 12,000 feet, getting round into sun as five 109's showed up. They began climbing with us into sun and our section went for them head-on. I saw tracer passing over my cockpit, engaged two 109's and began a climbing and turning match with them; we chased up to 20,000 feet and there was warm comfort in finding that my Spitfire could climb and turn inside the Messerschmitts with no trouble. At this height the Jerry No. 2 rolled over and dived away, his leader no doubt hoping that I would follow and that he could get on my tail; but this was an old dodge. When I went for him he too turned and dived away so smartly that I lost sight of him. During this show Morgan and the American, Norris, each shot down a Messerschmitt, but we lost two sergeants who baled out. The 109's had some useful cloud cover for their third party that day; we saw only their bombs dropping on Tamet and found our own ack-ack rather too accurate.

Back at Tamet the next day we came across some 109's and Stukas bombing our forward troops under cover of Macchi 202's at 13,000 feet. We went for the Macchis which stayed and fought. Well placed, with the sun behind us, I and my No. 2, Flight Sergeant Sales, dived on a couple of Italians 3,000 feet below; they did not spot us until we were on them and then they put down their noses to bolt for home but taking no evasive action. I took one and Sales the other; mine dived almost vertically to the deck. As we flew low over the ground my Spitfire gained easily and after several strikes the Macchi crashed, burst into flames and dissolved in bits and pieces.

Eventually we moved up to Tamet and settled in there; and it was at Tamet that I celebrated my twenty-first birthday.

We had three shows that day, the first a scramble after dawn stand-by when we saw only a lone 109 in the distance. After a quick lunch I went up with Pilot Officer Paul Brickhill, an Australian, who was later to be shot down and taken prisoner, and who is now a well-known author. We hoped to intercept two 109's but although we sighted them well below us, we lost them while we dived and I nearly passed out owing to lack of oxygen, fortunately noticing I needed it and turning it on in time.

On our third operation I led the squadron up to 13,000 feet from where we saw bombs bursting on Tamet and also five aircraft coming in from the sea. When we chased them, four began to dive but the fifth decided to climb; and with my No. 2, Pilot Officer McMahon, I went after it, another Macchi 202. When my cannons hit behind the cockpit, the pilot rolled the aircraft over and baled out, and I saw his parachute open nicely while his machine went down with pieces still breaking off. He was collected and found to be a *Maggiore* and commander of a Macchi squadron.

McMahon and I flew around for a time until we saw another Macchi low down; we dived out of the sun and began a long chase in and out of cloud, getting in a number of attacks. After putting up quite a fight, the Italian let down his flaps, crash-landed, and before the dust had settled, was out of the cockpit and darting away. I knew just how he felt. He was less fortunate than I, for he was taken prisoner.

He was, in fact, a *Colonello* and commanding officer of a Macchi gruppe, or wing; and I heard quite a bit about him subsequently from one of the Intelligence Officers who had interrogated him.

"Nice birthday present, those two you collected for us," the IO told me. "The colonel thinks you and Mac are quite sporting types for not shooting him up on the ground. It seems that the Eyeties take a fairly dim view of that sort of thing, and that it has been a topic in their mess from time to time."

"Did you get much from him?"

"A certain amount. He seemed a pretty good type, politely secure and all that. Apparently he's been in Africa for about fifteen months and has been a CO for about three."

"What does he think of the Jerries?"

"Not much. He says their pilots never think of attacking unless they've got everything in their favour. But if the odds are against them they dive or climb away, if they can. He thinks his own crowd are much better. He says they stay and fight it out, even though they've only got two guns."

"Does he like flying the Macchi?"

"Seemed to think it was all right, but he doesn't care for their r/t. Says it's poor and that when you shot him down his own was u/s. He also said that the only way his chaps can be sure of warning one another when there's trouble about is to waggle their wings."

Soon the war rolled away from Tamet as the big push for Tripoli continued, and we began to use thirty gallon overload tanks again, escorting bombing raids by Kittys on the Buerat-Gheddahia road, patrolling over our forward troops and covering tank battles and shelling. We moved again, to Wadi Surri, and from there patrolled the Tripoli-Castel Benito area.

During our first show over this area with twelve Spitfires at 18,000 feet, we saw some Ju-87 Stukas returning from bombing our troops. I reported them to our wing leader, Wing Commander Darwin, and dived down on them with the squadron following.

I felt rather exposed approaching the formation of Stukas on my own and for a time, until the squadron arrived, I had them all to myself, returning my fire and doing stall turns all round me. They were Italian Stukas and I caught up with them near Castel Benito aerodrome at about 1,000 feet. I shot at one without doing much damage but hit a second one in the starboard wing root, saw it burst into flames, spiral down and explode when it hit the ground.

"Nice show," said Darwin, when we got back to Wadi Surri. "I didn't see those chaps for a start. That makes your twelfth doesn't it?"

I said it did.

"Good show. Well, your promotion to Flight Lieutenant has come through. You'd better come over to my trailer to wet your new stripe this evening."

I was now a flight commander in 92 Squadron and enjoying life.

Tripoli was occupied on January 23rd and it seemed as though there might be a lull in the war for a couple of months. During this period we drove over to Misurata one day, bartered tea for eggs with the Arabs and cooked ourselves a meal of bully and eggs in a hotel. Ted Sly worked out a brilliant idea to augment our limited supplies of beer and whisky. He took an empty four gallon jerry can in his Spitfire on a trip to Castel

Benito, got the jerry filled with Chianti, and flew back with both feet on one rudder pedal to provide room for the can, fortunately meeting no 109's. The Chianti was good, even if it did taste a bit of petrol.

"Good enough to wet old Dukey's bar to the DFC." Ted Sly said, to my embarrassment. "Another 'immediate.' He's making a habit of it."

Mr Churchill arrived in Tripoli and there were various big parades; and one day McMahon and I were told to stand by for a secret job. It was to escort the Prime Minister to Malta in his Liberator; but we were not required after all. The squadron moved to Castel Benito airfield and though we enjoyed the change from the desert and relaxed in green and pleasant surroundings, life became rather quiet for a period for there was little flying. Wing Commander Gleed was the new commanding officer of the wing and Squadron Leader Peter Olver was the OC Flying.

A number of rumours began to float, one of them that sixty Focke Wulfs 190 were said to be at Gabes.

"My Gawd," Ted Sly sighed.

By March we were at Medanine and the war was on again, and there was nothing dull about life now. Morgan completed his tour and Squadron Leader Harper took over; while he was away for a period in Cairo on a course I was appointed acting-commanding officer and had an eventful week.

Once I was able to get two Macchi 202's during one sortie; both pilots baled out and I saw their parachutes going down together like a couple of mushrooms. Life was a bit hectic that evening for the Wehrmacht shelled our airfield at Medanine from the hills to the north-west and we were ordered to take-off immediately through the shell bursts and to land wherever we could. Two aircraft were damaged by shells and crashed on take-off, another crash-landed at Zuara; one Spit-fire of 145 Squadron got away with two pilots aboard, and the ground crew left *en masse*. I managed to put down at Castel Benito in the dark, thinking of Harper's parting words before he left:

"The squadron is in your hands!"

I reflected on his comment the following day. While taking-off with a section of four to do top cover to 145 over Gabes, there was some misunderstanding which resulted in one of the section wiping himself out in a head-on collision; and when we were airborne another had to turn back with engine trouble, leaving Flight Sergeant H Paterson and myself to carry on.

We went up to 22,000 feet, flew north of Gabes, and then set course for home in a gentle dive. While we were crossing the coast near the Mareth Line I saw a lone 109 F at about 10,000 feet, some 4,000 feet below us. As I dived and closed to about 250 yards, the 109 went up in a climbing turn to the left, but I managed to connect with cannons and machine-guns and he went straight down leaving a trail of smoke and breaking up.

This was a pretty busy period with the Battle of the Mareth Line progressing, and I was very fortunate in being able to get more 109's on each of three sorties. While leading seven of the squadron at 8,000 feet, I saw a couple of 109's coming our way, a little above us; our own ack-ack began to pepper them and, with Sergeant Askey as my No. 2, we went through the black puffs. My shells exploded behind the cockpit of the first Messerschmitt and the pilot baled out; we followed the second one down in a long chase, dodging ack-ack, and eventually saw him crash and explode.

During the next sortie—on a Sunday, and a lucky one for me this time—six of us patrolling over the Medanine area at 18,000 feet saw three 109's pass below us. They split up when we dived and I followed one in a climbing turn. After two bursts with cannons the aircraft appeared to lurch as though the pilot had been hit, and then went down in a wide spiral dive. That afternoon, with a section of four, we ran into about twenty 109's bound for the strip at Noffatia. Hunk and "Red" Chisholm both got one, and after another chase through our ack-ack, I caused the pilot to bale out from a 109 F.

It had been an eventful week and I was quite happy to hand over the squadron to Squadron Leader Harper when he returned from Cairo. We had lost several aircraft one way and another, and McMahon had been killed when he and Chisholm were picked on by seven Messerschmitts.

We also had a visitor, one of the Luftwaffe pilots I had shot down. He was wounded in the arm.

"He seems curious to meet you," said the IO.

He was a *Staffelführer,* the equivalent of a wing commander aged about twenty-four, and with an Iron Cross. We took him to the mess and chatted away about Spitfires and Messerschmitts, and, as he seemed a quite good type, we showed him the cockpit of a 5b.

Next day there was a terrific flap.

"Your Jerry has escaped," Harper told me.

Extra guards were mounted by all the aircraft in case he selected one for himself. But fortunately he did not get far; he was found in the camp wearing pyjamas.

The Battle of Mareth was won and 92 moved on again, this time to Bu Grara, a salt flat by the seashore where we had some trouble with aircraft sinking in the sand. To our immense satisfaction we went to Algiers on March 23rd to pick up some Spitfire 9's, a great improvement on the 5b, with more powerful engines; and one of our first operations with them was to patrol over the New Zealand Division making its left-hook to El Hamma. I have definite memories of this area, for while returning from a patrol between El Hamma and Gabes I chased a Junkers 88 and exchanged shots, travelling at round about 400 miles an hour. The rear-gunner put a bullet through one of my tyres and another through the airscrew; a couple more went into the leading edges of the wings. He got away, although damaged.

When Chisholm, who had been commander of B Flight, finished his tour he was succeeded by Hunk Humphreys, which pleased us for we were now both flight commanders of 92, an honour we appreciated.

"Duke, you are wanted on the telephone. It's the AOC, I think," I was told by Joe Cornish, our Intelligence Officer, one morning while on readiness during the push for Gabes.

"Probably going to tear you off a strip."

I picked up the receiver rather tentatively.

"Broadhurst here."

"Yes, sir."

"I thought you would like to know that you have been awarded an immediate DSO. Congratulations, Duke."

"Oh—er, thank you, sir."

When the news got around, Jerry Westenra came over from 601 Squadron and joined in a party which kept him with us until the following morning.

Two days later I was able to celebrate in another way. With a flight well north of Gabes we ran into six 109 G's with the sun at our backs; Doc Savage and I each got one, mine exploding on the ground near a German Red Cross, Hospital.

Gabes fell, the Army was on the way to Sfax; the Desert Air Force pressed on with patrols and sweeps and providing escorts for bombers. Since 92 had only a limited number of Spitfire 9's we flew usually with

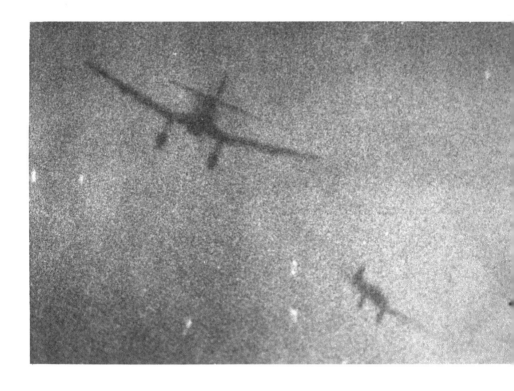

16.

The Ju 87's we attacked over Castel Benito, January 21st 1943.

17.

Ciné film of the Me 109F I shot down over Mareth, March 1943.

18.,

Tropicalized Spitfire Vb, 92 Squadron, Bir Dufan, 1943.

19.,

Instructor on Spitfire Vc, at Abu Suweir, 1943.

20.,

Sqn Ldr Sandy Kallio, my predecessor, 145 Squadron, 1944.

21.,

244 Wing, Venarro. Neville Duke, Sqn Ldr Graham Cox, Gp Capt Brian Kingcome, and Gp Capt Stan Turner.

22.

The Me 109F I shot down over Arezzo, May 13th 1944.

23.,

Some of my successful pilots in 145 Squadron. Back: Lt J Milborrow, Neville Duke, Flt Lt J Wooler; Front: FO J S Ekbury, Lt J S Anderson, Flt Sgt J Stirling. Between us we scored eight destroyed, one probable and one damaged; 21st May 1944.

four 9's as a top cover above eight 5b's; the 9's became lightly known as the "suicide" four for though they had a roving commission above the remainder of the formation and were expected to jump on any would-be attackers, they could also be jumped on and perhaps outnumbered by any 109's that might be higher still.

Sfax fell, and we went on to Fauconnerie, an airfield formerly used by the Luftwaffe, littered now with wrecks of 109's and FW-190's; and from Fauconnerie to Goubrine, near Sousse, where we welcomed the sight once again of green grass and flowers and birds.

The end of Rommel in North Africa was in sight; and there was one occasion when it was very nearly the end of Duke in North Africa, too.

I was leading a section of 9's at 20,000 feet as top cover to eight Spitfires from 145 Squadron headed by the wing leader, Wing Commander Gleed; we were on an offensive sweep over the Cape Bon area.

While scanning the sea I suddenly saw the shadows of a large number of aircraft on the water, though I could not see the actual aircraft. They were very low down and making for Tunis—Rommel's final reinforcements.

I called up Ian Gleed on the r/t and reported them.

"Can't see them from down here," he replied. "You lead on and we'll follow you."

My section followed me down and we soon sighted about eighteen Savoia 82's, three-engined transport aircraft. I selected one for attacking, but my machine was moving too quickly and I overshot. Throttling back, I attacked another, closed right up and skimmed over the top of him as he went into the sea, broke up and disappeared in masses of spray with the engine cowlings bouncing over the waves. I had time to shoot down another, which practically landed on the sea; and then a mixed formation of escorting Focke Wulfs and Messerschmitts appeared on the scene and jumped us.

Just as I was about to attack another Savoia I glanced back and found a Focke Wulf on my tail. And then, suddenly, the air seemed to be filled with Focke Wulfs. I saw one or two Spitfires leaving the area, and Ian Gleed's No. 2 bale out while his aircraft went down in flames. I had the Focke Wulfs to myself. This seemed to be it.

With the engine flat-out I flew low over the sea, twisting, turning, dodging, gaining a bit of confidence when I found that my Spit 9 could turn inside the Focke Wulfs, nearly blacking out sometimes with high G. Finally, in desperation and to get more height to fight, I put the aircraft into a steep climb and after what seemed a life-time found myself alone again.

When I got back I found that we had lost Ian Gleed. It was likely that he had found himself in my position, too, for he was heard calling for aid at one stage. It was a big loss; he had led the wing with great distinction. Within minutes of returning to base we were airborne again, sweeping the area led by Pete Olver in search for any sight of Ian Gleed. On the credit side we had collected about six Savoias. It was the opening act to one of the most amazing sights I was to see during the entire war.

The following evening 92 Squadron provided top cover to four American Kittyhawk and Warhawk squadrons, sweeping the Cape Bon area when they sighted a huge flight of Junkers 52 transports escorted by Messerschmitts on the way to Tunis. While we had to sit upstairs the Americans engaged and claimed fifty-eight Junkers and fourteen 109's.

Peering down from our cockpits occasionally we could see the Americans getting right in among the enemy, flying low over the sea. A Junkers would begin to glow, become a ball of flame, and stagger on over the water. Some went straight in, others succeeded in reaching land, only to crash and blow up.

As dusk fell we looked down to see burning aircraft glowing over an area of many square miles. It was a blood-chilling sight.

This slaughter continued for several days. A South African squadron met up with fifteen Junkers and shot down every one with one loss to themselves. The Germans also had some successes; our losses included six among the Americans, three each by 92 and 601; and 145 lost five when they were jumped by twenty-five Messerschmitts.

The Eighth Army offensive on Enfidaville now began, and we were kept busy covering, sweeping, patrolling, delousing; once we covered three destroyers on the way to Tunis; another time we escorted 120 Mitchells bombing Pantellaria.

Officially I was now just about "OTE"—operational tour expired, but I managed to get as much flying as possible and I was still on operations when Tunis and Bizerta fell. I was pleased, and proud, to have been able to remain to the end.

I completed my last operation of my second tour on May 11th. We flew around Cape Bon during the afternoon, escorting American Kittyhawks on a bombing raid.

When the bombs had gone down the controller called up all aircraft.

"Return to base. The show is over." he said.

It was the final operation of the North African campaign.

With my second tour ended I began to hope that I should be able to spend my leave in Kent, especially as various people including several high-ranking officers had assured me that I was now certain of a posting home. It was wonderful to think about.

I was also very pleased when Hunk Humphreys was appointed commanding officer of 92 Squadron. Several of us had finished operations for the time being and there were many mess parties, some of which were hilarious and spirituous, particularly one before I set off on the long haul back to Cairo.

Returning by stages, I made quite an eager entry at the RAF Headquarters, Middle East, keen to learn when I might take-off for England. I was told to come back the next morning. That evening I reflected that I had been in the battle for the Agheila Line, the Buerat Line, the Mareth Line and the final push for Tunis. On my second tour I had managed to collect fourteen enemy aircraft, making a total of twenty-two, and probably damaged or destroyed others. My operational hours for the second tour were two hundred and two, making a total of four hundred and twenty-four for two tours in two hundred and ninety-three sorties.

Back at headquarters next morning I was received by a frosty wing commander.

"Nobody is going home," he said.

I explained that I had been told by the C-in-C that I would be going; the wing commander told me to return during the afternoon. I went away, quite happily, feeling that I should soon be seeing England. I had lunch at the Ghezira with Hunk, on leave after a course, and several other types; we swam and drank. Life was good.

This cheerfulness was soon shattered. The wing commander confirmed that I was staying in the Middle East and said that I had been recommended for a staff job as squadron leader. I argued my way out of that one; but when it was suggested that I might return to El Ballah I became temporarily speechless.

I had a lot to drink that night from sheer disappointment and, since I was to stay in the Middle East, I would have given much to have found myself back again with 92. By the middle of June I was on rest tour, this time as a squadron leader and chief flying instructor at 73 OTU, Abu Suweir, near Ismailia. I felt at least this was definitely preferable to a staff job.

## CHAPTER 7

# *Italy*

---

THE sun was still low over the horizon of the desert but occasionally as I weaved, looking for aircraft to attack, its rays glinted on the wings of my Spitfire 5b the tips of which were painted white. I had taken off just as dawn was breaking and at any moment I could expect a dog-fight. I sighted a vic of three Spitfires and went over and down to get on their tails; they saw me and split up and I began a climbing match with them as I had done so often against 109's. But now there would be no firing, no crashing or baling out; this was just part of the course at No. 73 Operational Training Unit at Abu Suweir, the white wing-tips of my Spitfire indicating to the pupils in the three Spitfires that they had been jumped on by their instructor.

Despite that bout of disappointment in Cairo at not going home for leave, I was enjoying life as Chief Flying Instructor, responsible for training Spitfire pilots particularly in air combat and fighter tactics before they went on to join the Desert Air Force. There was a routine for each Course to follow: training in a Harvard before going solo in a Spitfire, flying in battle formation, attacks on bomber formations, ground strafing, examinations. And this practice dogfighting which became a popular sport, with the pupils trying to jump their CFI, was one of the most enjoyable parts of the course, particularly for me. It meant regular flying, keeping my hand in for my third tour, and was infinitely preferable to any staff job.

During the heat of the summer we worked from dawn until midday, and when the sun was at its height we had a siesta and then went swimming or sailing in the Suez Canal or the Great Bitter Lakes. There was a pattern and routine about life as each Course arrived, went through its training, left and was succeeded by another. If there was tedium in correcting examination papers there was also plenty of flying;

and at the end of each Course we would have a mass exercise when our Spitfires and their experienced pupils intercepted mock bombing and strafing of dummy ground targets by Kittyhawks, targets which might be the Suez Canal, or Port Said, or old tanks and lorries.

These exercises had their moments. Once while I was leading twelve Spitfires mock-attacking oil refineries at Suez, my No. 2, a South African, misjudged his distance over the glassy, calm surface of the Gulf of Suez, an easy thing to do. He hit the sea, flying at about 300 miles an hour, bounced high but ditched skilfully and successfully, and I circled above him until he was picked up by an Egyptian fishing boat, shaken but intact. Once a Kittyhawk, taking-off with a section on exercise, struck a taxiing Spitfire whose pilot was killed instantly. The Spitfire continued to taxi in circles and I had to chase it, climb aboard, grope into the cockpit and switch off the engine.

Sometimes we had co-operation exercises with torpedo Beaufighters and Wellingtons from the Coastal Command Training School at Shalufa, usually accompanied by realistic dog-fights between Kittyhawks and Spitfires, some of them a little too realistic. A diversion was a visit by King Peter, of Yugoslavia, who stayed with us to qualify for his RAF wings and was passed out by the Station Commander, Group Captain John Grandy, DSO, after a satisfactory performance with a Harvard.

With a number of Desert Air Force pilots at Abu Suweir on rest there was plenty of good company. Ted Sly, the Australian, was instructor to one of the three Spitfire flights; I shared a bungalow with Squadron Leader Geoff Garton, DFC, who had flown Hurricanes during the Battle of France in 1940; the Station Adjutant, Flight Lieutenant Bunny Isaac, was another Desert man and one of his possessions was a big German Horsch car which he had managed to loot somewhere or other and which was most valuable for reaching the fleshpots of Cairo occasionally, eighty miles away. We also had an old Hawker Hart and a Fairchild Argus cabin aircraft which served for reaching Cairo and Alexandria—and once for landing in the desert to pick up Ted Sly and two WAAF officers.

One day while I was in Cairo I saw a familiar figure.

It was Brian Kingcome, whom I had not seen since he had gone on rest from Biggin Hill. He was now, I noticed, a Group Captain.

"What brings you here, sir?" I asked.

"Spot of leave from Italy."

"What are you doing there?"

"I've got 244 Wing. Let's have a drink."

We had a grand reunion, starting at Shepherd's and continuing at the Turf Club, Jimmy's Bar, the Continental, and various other places.

While we were sipping our beer I said to Brian:

"I suppose you haven't got a place in your wing for me?"

"As a matter of fact," Brian replied, "I've already asked for you. I wanted you for taking over 92 when Hunk Humphreys finished his second tour, but it seemed you're still supposed to be resting."

I was pleased to know that he had asked for me, but disappointed at not being able to succeed Hunk.

"Who has the squadron now?"

"Chap named Mackie, a New Zealander. Damn good type. They call him Rosie because of his fresh, pink face."

"Any hope of my succeeding him?"

"Could be. We'll see."

I went down to Heliopolis to see Brian off for Italy. He was getting a lift in General Montgomery's DC3; but as we were roaring on to the airfield, making sure to be punctual, we saw the General's aircraft taking off. He had arrived ten minutes before schedule and was in a hurry.

The months ticked by at Abu Suweir, Course succeeded Course, and I began to get restless to return to operations. My posting to the Desert Air Force in Italy came through at the end of February, 1944. A round of farewell parties, take-off from Cairo West in a DC3 at dawn, landings at El Adem and Malta just two and a quarter years since I had last been in Malta believing that I should be back again in England in six weeks— and then on to Catania, in Sicily, landing finally at Capodichino, near Naples. I had nearly caught up with the war again: the front line was a little north of Naples and because of the winter and for other reasons, there was a temporary full stop at Cassino.

I went straight to the Base Personnel Depot and hearing that Squadron Leader Mackie was about, sought him out. He had finished his tour with 92 Squadron a few days earlier and had been succeeded by Squadron Leader Graham Cox. So I had missed out on 92 Squadron. Mackie, who like Cox, had the DSO and DFC, told me that 92 had been in Malta for a while when Hunk had been CO. It had taken part in the invasion of Sicily, and had been based there for a while; and, with

Mackie succeeding Hunk, it had been active in various places including Salerno. It was now at Marcianise with 244 Wing, near Caserta.

I rang up Brian Kingcome.

"You're coming to this wing," he said. "Can't let you have 92, but I've got an appointment for you. I'll have you picked up tomorrow morning."

On the drive to Marcianise, bumping along the muddy Italian roads in the rain, I wondered what "the job" might be. I reported to Brian and, over lunch with his wing commander flying, a Canadian, Stan Turner, DSO, DFC, together with a visitor, Wing Commander Warburton, DSO, DFC, a distinguished photographic reconnaissance pilot, I thought about my new posting. I was to take over 145 Squadron; its commanding officer, Squadron Leader Sandy Kallio, DFC, another Canadian, had broken a leg crash-landing a Spitfire. After lunch Warburton left for England in a Lockheed P38 and was not heard of again. He went missing somewhere off Gibraltar.

Before Brian introduced me to 145 Squadron there was one thing I wanted to do: meet up again with the boys in 92. It was good to see all the old ground crew again, still the same as they had been at Biggin and in North Africa; many of the pilots I knew, for they had passed through Abu Suweir. Dear old Joe Cornish, the Intelligence Officer, brought me up to date with all the news, and my first glimpse of Graham Cox, the CO, was while he was giving some of the pilots a sharp address about various "blacks" that had been put up during a party at Caserta Palace the previous evening.

I took an immediate liking to Graham, particularly when, with the height of hospitality, he let me take up one of 92's Spitfires for a look around the sector; I flew over the Cassino foothills, Naples and Vesuvius, careful not to get the wrong side of the lines for the moment. Graham put me up for the night. I felt at home again.

The next morning Brian Kingcome took me to meet the commanding officers of 601 and 417 Squadrons, the latter Canadian, and then we went on to 145. We ploughed through thick mud (which seemed about two feet deep) to the mess, a captured Italian tent shared by the pilots of all ranks, and found all the officers and pilots assembled there.

I felt rather self-conscious. Every new commanding officer of a squadron is regarded with critical, appraising eyes during the first few moments of his introduction, and not a word or a movement is missed but noted carefully; during the first few days he is usually treated with great reserve. I wondered how I should make out.

Unfortunately, I was not to be too popular with the squadron during those early days. The commanding officer had a car allotted to him, and more than usual significance was attached to that run by the CO of 145. It was a huge Lancia, "liberated" in Sicily, pride of the pilots, who piled into it in large numbers and made off for Naples whenever they could for parties and the bright lights.

Very soon after my arrival I went into Naples with Graham Cox and Wing Commander Teddy Morris, who had commanded 250 Squadron in the desert while I was with 112. We drove in this splendid vehicle.

The evening began badly. Teddy Morris, in his best blues, and in animated conversation, did not see a hole, fully six feet deep and filled with mud and water; he walked slap into it. We hauled him out, scraped his uniform as clean as we could, and fixed him up with a mixed set of blues. We had an enjoyable evening at the Officers' Club and left, in pouring rain, to pick up the Lancia from which I had carefully removed the rotor arm to immobilize it.

Where we had parked the Lancia was now a vacant gap. Somebody had evidently been around with another rotor arm and had re-liberated the squadron's magnificent car. I feel it is best to draw a screen over that long walk back in the rain to the camp. There was a touch of frost about the atmosphere in the mess during the following days. Far too many people found themselves unable to get to Naples.

I was fortunate in having a first class adjutant in "Adj" Brown, from the Isle of Man, who took all the administrative weight of the squadron and left me free to concentrate on the flying—he was almost fatherly in his attitude.

I turned my attention to the squadron's Spitfires. They were 8's, to my mind one of the finest Mark of Spitfire ever produced. They carried two 20 mm cannons, four .303 machine-guns, were fitted with Merlin 45 or 46 engines, and could more than hold their own with the Me-109 and the FW-190 although the "long nose" Focke Wulf with Daimler-Benz engines was a formidable aircraft.

Brian Kingcome gave me the form about the work 244 Wing was doing.

"Our job," he said, "is to give air cover over Anzio where the Army has got a bridgehead. That cover is continuous from dawn to dusk, and one squadron relieves another. It takes half an hour to reach Anzio and each squadron does half an hour over the area. The squadron which finishes its patrol at dusk does not return here, but stays at Nettuno for the night and goes up again at dawn until it is relieved and returns here. The Jerries shell Nettuno most of the time, so the pilots spend their nights in dug-outs and hope to wake up and find that their aircraft have not been hit."

"What height do we patrol at?"

"About 15,000 feet, in eights or twelves. You'll have to watch out for 190's and 109's. Their idea is to make as many bombing and strafing attacks on the Army as possible."

Maintaining this standing patrol over Anzio called for good organization, with squadrons starting up at exact times, taking off in pairs, forming up into two or three flights of four aircraft in box formation, climbing out over the coast and heading round Gaeta Point to Anzio. No patrol could leave the bridgehead area until it was relieved.

I did my first patrol, the first operation of my third tour, on March 4th, 1944, the day after taking over command of 145, whose score of enemy aircraft destroyed was one hundred and ninety-six. There was a lot of cloud about and we did not see much. I felt rather like a new boy again after my long absence from operations, but it was good to be back.

We saw plenty of Anzio in the following weeks. The area was plastered with shell holes, and the only activity we could see below was the flashing of guns. There were times when we fairly tore up to the bridge-head, listening to the ground controller reporting bandits approaching Anzio and being engaged by the squadron we were to relieve. Sometimes we arrived to join in the scrap, but usually the Luftwaffe had gone by the time we got there. The beachhead area was not large and practice was needed to position ourselves over the patrol line and at the same time take advantage of the sun when it appeared, so that we should be between it and any visitors.

Flak spouted up in spate. My second day as CO of 145 might easily have been my last. A shell splinter punched a hole in my starboard wing the size of my head and only a few inches away from the cannon ammunition, peppering the radio with bits and pieces and damaging the leading edge of the wing.

Whenever we could, we used to sweep up to Rome to have a look round, to the irritation of the Wehrmacht which sent flak up too close for comfort.

The Army was endeavouring to push past Cassino and to link up with the bridgehead at Anzio; and in the middle of March, on a clear, sunny day, we took off to patrol over the area during the big bombing raid which flattened the famous monastery and was intended for softening up the German defences. When we arrived over Cassino, cloud closed down to 6,000 feet; we sat under it, watching bombing by Kittyhawks and artillery fire winking as a terrific barrage was laid down; Cassino was a mass of bomb craters and shell holes, shrouded in smoke. The Germans held on, and returning the following day, we watched further artillery fire and were well content to be high above it. At this time the squadron raised its score to two hundred and our IO, Dave Ker, was kept busy.

We continued to patrol Anzio and Cassino; as well as offensive sorties. We escorted bombing raids on the Orvieto marshalling yards. In a raid on an ammunition dump in the Valmontore area south-east of Rome American Bostons must have secured a direct hit—the earth just lifted in a sheet of flame. During March my operational hours totted up to forty; and since in theory a tour was restricted to 180 hours, Brian Kingcome ordered me to ration my flying.

April passed and the wing was moved to Venafro, not far from Cassino, nearer the front and in preparation for the expected push for Rome. The second battle for Cassino began on May 11th with a barrage of 2,000 guns, the air rent with the din, the sky lit with flashes at night. Two days later I led six Spitfires from 145 on a sweep over the Perugia area. We were at extreme range and feeling rather lonely deep in enemy territory.

It was worthwhile; we destroyed three 109's and damaged three more. I had with me two South Africans, Lieutenants F M Du Toit and S M Greene; a Rhodesian, Flight Lieutenant W A R Macdonald; and Flight Lieutenant C R Parbury and Flight Sergeant D H Lorimer.

We sighted the Messerschmitts while we were at 17,000 feet, south of Arezzo. They were to the north of us, about 500 feet below and we turned and chased them. Macdonald and Lorimer got one each, Parbury and Greene damaged two more and I was able to hit one before it dived away.

Climbing back to rejoin my section I saw a Messerschmitt circling above me, and we went into the routine of a climbing and turning bout. My aircraft had the edge on him and, at 14,000 feet, just as I was about to open fire, the 109 throttled back, skidded, and slipped into a stalled position, evidently hoping that I would overshoot so that he could take up an attacking position. But I was able to fire from a range of about one hundred to one hundred and fifty yards; large pieces broke off from the Messerschmitt, which dropped away in a wide spiral and went into the ground.

Luck was with us again the following day when, in addition to Greene and Lorimer, I had with me two more South Africans, Lieutenants D J Beisieger and J S Anderson, and three of our flight sergeants, R W McKernan, W Hughes and A G Newman. While over the Cassino area after returning from a sweep up to Rome and Perugia, the controller reported eight 109's above and some distance behind us. We found them two hundred feet above, all carrying bombs, which they dropped as soon as they saw us and which may have landed on their own troops since we were over enemy territory. As they dived we chased after them; Beisieger and I got one each, and Lorimer, McKernan and Greene damaged three more.

Although we continued to patrol over the Cassino battle area we saw no more enemy aircraft for three or four days; they did, however, make an attempt to bomb our airfield at Venafro, and we countered by sweeping over their aerodromes round Lake Bolsena, taking off before dawn after a restless night at Nettuno on the Anzio beachhead. Flying Officer Ekbury shot down one of a section forming up over the lake; the others dodged into cloud.

As a result of various squadrons being shuffled to Anzio and Venafro, 145 was attached to 324 Wing at Lago, south of the Volturno, commanded by Group Captain Duncan Smith, DSO, DFC, whose wing leader was Wing Commander Du Vivier, DFC, an outstanding Belgian pilot. This wing included 111 Squadron, led by Hunk Humphreys who was also on his third tour, and Nos. 43, 72 and 93. As visitors, the pilots of 145 Squadron were keen to prove themselves, and the opportunity occurred after a day on readiness at Nettuno.

Before returning to Lago eight aircraft from 145 were detailed to escort twenty-four Baltimores of the USAAF and to give them area cover over Velletri where their bombs were scheduled for the enemy support lines. I led one box of four and the other was headed by one of my flight commanders, Flight Lieutenant Jock Wooler. While we were at about 15,000 feet on course to meet up with the Baltimores Jock called up on the radio:

"190's. Two o'clock above."

We had met up abruptly with about eighteen Focke Wulfs, all carrying bombs, with a top cover of 109's ranging up to about 17,000 feet.

The 190's were in three sections, line abreast; we turned starboard towards them and tore into the leading section from the stern quarter. I hit one with a burst from short range; it went down in a mass of flames, and after a quick weave to port another of this section came within my sights. The Spitfire's explosive ammunition seemed to produce stars over the 190's fuselage, the hood flew off and out shot the pilot. There was no time to see whether his parachute had opened for the remaining Focke Wulfs, after getting rid of their bombs, went off in all directions and dived for the north, several followed by Spitfires on their tails. I selected a pair and went after them in a long chase until accurate and heavy flak decided me to turn away. I was now entirely alone with no other aircraft in sight, but after weaving about and watching for any stragglers I met our Baltimores returning from their target and joined up with them, as much for the protection they could give me as for any I could give them.

The squadron returned to Lago in ones and twos until there were seven; the eighth was my No. 2 Flying Officer Somers, a good and experienced pilot who had been with 145 for many months. I waited for him at dispersal for hours, but we never heard anything of him again and nobody knew what had happened to him. He was the first and only No. 2 I lost throughout the war.

The brighter side of the picture was that eight of us had shot down eight Focke Wulfs, probably destroyed another and damaged two: Wooler, Ekbury, Lieutenants Jeff Milborrow and Anderson and Flight Sergeant Stirling each getting one. We felt it had been a good introduction to 324 Wing.

Towards the end of May the push began from Anzio to link up with the advance from Cassino; we were kept busy and frequently flew far north of Rome. 145 returned to 244 Wing; and Brian Kingcome sent for me after escorting twenty-four Bostons over the Frascati area.

"Party tonight," he said.

"Good show. Any particular reason?"

"To celebrate the second bar to your DFC," he replied cheerfully.

"I'll give the party," I declared.

But in the end the squadron insisted on giving it for me; and it was quite a party. The Squadron MO, stocky and tough "Doc" Brennan, Irish and a boxer, was useful next morning.

Three days later, on June 6th, we were cheered by the news that the invasion of Normandy had begun.

On June 7th I decided to take Mackenzie, Milborrow and Anderson off on a strafing expedition in the Rieti area, the first operation of its kind that the wing had attempted. We located some trucks and set them on fire but I found that my radiator had been hit, either by flak or by bullets from my own machine ricocheting off the ground. The engine began to vibrate and flames started to shoot out from the exhaust stubs as I pulled up and gained some height.

I turned for home, losing height, but keeping the aircraft going by slowly opening the throttle and then closing it quickly when the flames began to shoot again. Smoke began to fill the cockpit and I realized that I should have to bale out.

Seeing a break in the low clouds, I went through it to find Lake Bracciano about 2,000 feet below; the lake is nine miles across and I had arrived over the centre. The smoke in the cockpit became excessive and the engine was well on fire; I released my safety straps and the oxygen connections, rolled the aircraft on its back travelling at about 180 miles an hour, and expected to fall clear. Whether or not it was my preoccupation with the smoke I am not sure, but I realized too late that I had only slid back and not jettisoned the cockpit hood. Now my parachute was caught—preventing me from dropping out, and I was very low.

It was quite unpleasant to be hanging there upside down, half-in and half-out, with the nose of the Spitfire beginning to drop; and seeing, through smoke and flames, the lake coming up at me with alarming speed. I put in some concentrated kicking and eventually fell clear to feel my helmet and oxygen mask ripped away from my head by the slipstream.

The relief of being free of the aircraft and the sensation of falling head over heels were so pleasant that a few seconds passed before I thought of pulling the rip-cord. When I jerked the ring the parachute opened quickly, so quickly in fact, as I was moving rather fast, that one of the shoulder straps broke or came undone, causing me to fall half-out of the harness. I managed to pull myself back into it, still clutching the parachute ring; and with a sense of peculiar detachment while swinging from side to side I saw where my Spitfire had crashed into the lake and noticed that I was drifting towards the northern shore where, since their retreat from Rome had begun, I imagined there would be many Germans.

I felt that I was falling slowly until I was fairly near the water, and then it appeared to rush towards me; and as I splashed into it I banged the release box and everything except one leg strap dropped clear. But this one leg strap kept me fastened to the parachute, which seemed to have no intention of settling on the lake but of tearing madly over it, blown by the wind. As a result, I was dragged over the water, and then began to go under it and to swallow a large quantity until I was threshing around, beginning to think that I should be drowned. The parachute settled on the lake and began to sink rapidly, and now, with the leg strap still holding me, to drag me under. With a sudden inspiration I slipped the dinghy with the quick release and decided to rely on my Mae West; I bobbed quickly to the surface, coughing and spluttering.

The water seemed quite warm, and when I had got back my breath I looked up to see the remainder of my section circling above. I began to swim.

After about twenty minutes I noticed a boat put out from the shore. Italians? Or Germans?

As it drew nearer I saw there were two boys in it, and from their voices decided that they were Italians. They were. They helped me to scramble into the boat and set off for the side of the lake as fast as they could go.

We were met by several peasant farmers, and, after some sign language and broken English, we went up a hill at a sharp trot, because it was quite plain that they were scared of Germans arriving. When we reached a wood they helped me to remove my wet clothes, which they hid hastily, and one by one presented me with alternative garments. By the time I had put them on I looked a sight. The trouser legs reached nearly up to my knees, the coat came half way up my arms, and the hat perched on the top of my head. We grinned at one another cheerfully and then, in case any inquisitive Germans might arrive, we lay low for a while; fortunately I was safe, for the Wehrmacht had withdrawn a couple of hours before, our people had not yet advanced, and we were in an area of temporary no man's land.

When the Italians decided we could move safely, we set off along the lakeside, moving with a good deal of care, until we reached a house.

"Vino," one of them grinned at me.

"Grazie," I replied cheerfully.

Vino—and bread and cheese and tea—were soon set in front of me, and while I munched away it seemed that half the population of the neighbourhood began to arrive to look me over furtively. They laughed and chatted among themselves and I was eventually shown to a bedroom and settled down for a sleep.

"Hey, bud, wake up!"

I looked up to see two Americans with tommy-guns and a threatening manner. And that was the beginning of a hectic return to Venafro. At various stages along the way, the Italians gave me receptions when I seemed to be surrounded by masses of flowers and wine glasses that would never empty; and in Rome I spent a wonderful night, ending up by sleeping under an American lorry for lack of anything better. The following morning I was given a lift to Aquino in a Piper Cub, and from there covered the last stage to Venafro in a Fairchild. Brian and the squadrons seemed pleased to have me back and there was another party. Apart from a bruised right thigh caused by the parachute, and one or two twinges of cramp which came from wandering about in wet socks and shoes, I felt fine. As a memento I still had my parachute ring—which now hangs in our lounge at Dunsfold—and the mild distinction of being one of the few pilots to bale out and land in fresh water during the war.

The next few days were spent in resting, sunbathing and occasionally swimming in the Volturno with Graham Cox, who at one stage of my visit to Lake Bracciano had wanted to fly over and drop me packets of money. We had a few days and a few parties in Rome, and returned to join the advance.

The wing moved on to Fabrica, near Lake Vico, north of "Duke's Folly" (Lake Bracciano), set in pleasant country with a climate cooler than Rome. Wing Commander Turner finished his tour and was replaced by Wing Commander "Cocky" Dundas, DSO, DFC; we had lost three pilots and seven or eight aircraft during strafing operations.

With the Germans retreating north of Rome, and a sharp falling off in Luftwaffe activity, the wing began a new role; our Spitfires were fitted with racks to carry a 500 lb bomb, and after practising dive bombing at sixty degrees over the sea we began operating, securing results which were agreed to be effective on a number of targets. This bombing was not without its occupational hazards, however, and it was dangerous when the bombs hung up and we could not release them. The South African Du Toit was killed when a bomb would not release but fell off and exploded when he landed, blowing his aircraft to pieces and killing him instantly. He was a fine chap and it was very bad luck. Once, while attacking a level crossing north of Bologna, my bomb hung up during a dive and fell off while I was dodging round some trees avoiding flak, exploding under the aircraft and throwing it about so violently that I thought the flak had connected.

From Fabrica we moved on to Perugia, and from a good aerodrome with a short concrete runway and a generous grass strip our bombs began to fall around Faenza, Forli and Rimini. There were one or two bad accidents at Perugia: a Marauder bomber force-landed after being badly shot up, hitting one of our Spitfires in a dispersal area; both aircraft became a mass of flames and the pilot, being unable to get out from the cockpit, was burned to death. Two of his crew were badly burned and one died later. On another occasion an aircraft of 417 Squadron overshot on landing, bounced into the dispersal area and wrote off two Spitfires.

Frequently we ran into accurate flak which seemed to follow us around the sky despite all our attempts to dodge it. It was, in fact, predicted 88 mm flak, fired from some half a dozen guns, and when we were caught by a box of these infernal machines there were moments that seemed like hours, with the aircraft feeling as though it were standing still, the Germans trying to anticipate our every move as we changed direction and height. Flak was becoming one of the biggest menaces; and the Wehrmacht also developed a habit of not using tracer with their light 20 and 30 mm and machine-gun fire so that we should not know that we were being given a reception while going down on a target.

There were several moments of pleasant relaxation: a dinner in the town of Perugia when the entire 145 Squadron sat down at one table; visits to Assisi for a bath and dinner; and a trip to Ferno and a bathe in the Adriatic.

Another diversion was to take the squadron over to Rosignano for, with 92, we had been ordered to link up with the forces taking part in the invasion of Southern France. On August 15th, equipped with drop tanks, we did an early morning patrol over the Franco-Italian coastline border in case fighters should come up from Milan and Turin to attack swarms of gliders making for the beachhead. We had a wonderful view of the Alps in the early morning light. The Luftwaffe stayed at home. After further uneventful patrols, I went over to Corsica for a closer look at the invasion and, meeting Graham Cox, to whom the same idea had occurred, landed with him on an advanced strip at Ramatuelle, near St Tropez, passing over a mass of shipping and balloons. A dusty, crowded strip was being used by 324 Wing, which included 111 Squadron, still led by Hunk. The following morning I flew No. 2 to Wing Commander Heath, with Graham Cox as No. 2 to Hunk Humphreys, on a sweep of the Valence-Lyons area in the hope of seeing 109's; and, after a drive along the Riviera towards Cannes with Hunk and Graham, returned to Perugia.

With the final battle for the Gothic Line, our wing moved to Loreto, south of Ancona, and it was from this airfield near the sea that I managed to shoot down my last two aircraft during the war. We had the notion to put up aircraft before first light in an attempt to catch 109's on reconnaissance down the Adriatic coast.

Accompanied by Flying Officer J Hamer as my No. 2 I took off before dawn to patrol the battle area between Pesaro and Rimini. There was nothing to be seen over the battle area, and not wishing to attract our own ack-ack, we flew north of Ancona along the coast at about 10,000 feet. Control reported two bogeys north-west of Pesaro, 3,000 feet above us; we missed them in cloud but picked them up north of Rimini—three 109's flying in line abreast.

All three put on full boost immediately they saw us, clouds of black smoke coming from their engines. Hamer and I went after them and when the port aircraft lagged slightly I opened up at long range, about six hundred to eight hundred yards, producing a bright flash on his fuselage. After I had drawn closer and fired again, the hood of the 109 flew off and out came the pilot. The two remaining Germans dived and then climbed steeply to 14,000 or 15,000 feet, a height at which we were able to use the Spitfire's supercharger; and so we caught them easily. I selected one and, firing from long range, closed to two hundred yards. The aircraft caught fire and again the pilot baled out. The third 109 disappeared. It may have been that all three of the German pilots were reconnaissance men only for they took little avoiding action and no advantage of cloud. We did hear that I was reputed by the Germans to have shot down one of their leading pilots at about this time, but I can recall no interesting fights. He may have been one of these two lads.

The wing moved again, to Fano, further up the coast towards Rimini; and my operational hours were running out. From Fano we did several "Rover Davids", a cab-rank system, when six, eight, or twelve bombed-up Spitfires patrolled over the front line; and controlled by an RAF officer with the troops in a forward position, were directed on to targets. Sometimes the Army fired green smoke-shells over targets to be bombed, such as gun positions. There were also armed reconnaissances round Ravenna, Ferrara and Ostliglia; flak and some losses could always be expected, one of our Spitfires diving straight into the ground after being hit, others crash-landing.

"Your tour ends with this month. AOC's orders," Brian Kingcome informed me one day.

The AOC was Air Chief Marshal Dickson; September was running out. Although I was restricted to flying once a day, I managed to get in four more dawn flights in the hope of sighting more 109's; but there were none about.

My final operations were on September 20th, a dawn recce above Rimini when I sighted a lone Wellington; and a cab-rank during the afternoon when we bombed and straffed where some tanks were reported, securing four out of six strikes in the target area. When we returned to Fano the weather was clamping down and rain was falling.

"The AOC has ordered that your tour is to end immediately," Brian told me next morning. "You have flown more hours than he thought. 145 will be taken over by Squadron Leader Daniels tomorrow. It seems pretty certain that you will be going back to England."

I had, in fact, done two hundred and eighty-eight hours on operations for my third tour during one hundred and ninety-three sorties. This brought my total operational period for the three tours to seven hundred and twelve hours, with four hundred and eighty-six sorties. I had flown for five hundred and ninety-three hours on operations with the Desert Air Force, and my score of enemy aircraft was twenty-eight destroyed, three probably destroyed, and five damaged.

There was the usual small ceremony when I handed over 145 to

Daniels, but though I had prepared a set speech I found that all I could say to the squadron was: "Thanks."

Various farewell parties followed and visits to Florence and Sorrento. Brian took me to see Air Chief Marshal Dickson, who said that he had recommended that I should return to England. Soon I was waiting in Naples for a posting. It came through on October 27th—for the United Kingdom.

Four days later I took off from Pymigliano in a Dakota with one of my flight commanders, Frankie Banner, DFC, who was also tour expired, just three days short of three years after I had left Plymouth for Cairo. We flew out over Anzio, crossed Corsica, Toulon, Marseilles, Le Havre and landed at Lyneham at 5.30 pm. I was driven to Swindon where I missed a train connection to London, and it took me longer to get from Swindon to Tonbridge than it had to fly to Lyneham from Pymigliano.

All the buses had stopped when I reached Tonbridge eventually; I left my bags at the station and walked to Hadlow Road. I felt it was much too late to wake my father and mother, and decided to slip into the house through a back window, go to bed in my old room and greet the folks at breakfast.

But the window was locked, and in the end I had to knock at the front door, adding a whistle so that my mother might not be alarmed at being awakened at such an hour. Mother recognized my whistle, and in a very short time she and my father and Peggy—all in their dressing gowns— were plying me with questions in the lounge.

My room was unchanged from the day I had gone to Uxbridge; the dust sheet still lay over the model aerodrome.

It was good to be home again.

## CHAPTER 8

# *Glimpsing the Future*

---

I SPENT my leave at home in Tonbridge, with occasional trips up to London, and it was more than pleasant to be back again with the family and to meet many old friends. Although my three years away had seemed a long time while I was out of England, now they appeared to have just flitted by; and it was often difficult, while sitting in front of the fire at home chatting, to realize that I had been away at all.

As the days went by I wondered from time to time what the Air Ministry proposed to do with me. In my own mind I was certain of two things: that I did not want to become "chairborne" in some office; but that, while I wanted to continue flying if possible, I was not keen to become an instructor again.

When I called at Postings in the Air Ministry I said my little piece to that effect, and I was heard with consideration.

"How would you like to try your hand at production testing?" I was asked. "We have a scheme for attaching pilots on operational rest to aircraft manufacturing firms. The job is to test-fly new aircraft off the production line."

There was nothing chairborne about this. I could continue to fly. I said I was interested.

"We'll see what we can arrange and get in touch with you."

So off I went; and a few days later I received a note telling me to call on Philip Lucas, chief test pilot of Hawker Aircraft at Langley, near Slough, in Buckinghamshire. I went down to Langley on November 18th, less than three weeks after my return from Italy, and there I met Philip Lucas, George Bulman, who had been chief test pilot before Lucas and was now a director of the company, Bill Humble, the No. 2 test pilot, and several other people.

As far as I could tell, the interview seemed to go off satisfactorily;

Lucas explained the attachment scheme to me and said that most of the production testing would be on Tempest 2's and 5's. I had not seen a Tempest before—they were not even flying when I had been in England last—and I remember thinking that the Tempest 2 looked very much like a Focke Wulf 190 when Bill Humble took me out to have a look at one. The Fury, most secret at that time, was hidden behind screens in the experimental hangar.

After this instructive morning, Bill Humble offered me a lift to London in his car. Having said goodbye to him, the first person I ran into was Jamie Rankin, whom I had not seen since the Biggin days, and also Stan Turner, not long back from Italy; we did a round of the clubs ending up at six o'clock the next morning!

A couple of days later, while I was still catching up on my lost sleep, a telegram arrived from the Air Ministry. It said that I would be posted to Hawker's at Langley from January 1st, 1945 to January 1st, 1946. My rank would be Flight Lieutenant. I was quite content to drop from Squadron Leader; and though one of the suggestions for my future was that I should be posted as Wing Commander, Assistant Air Attaché at Chunking, I preferred to continue flying.

One point had to be settled, however; what was to be done with me between the end of November and the beginning of January. Someone suggested at the Air Ministry that I might do a lecture tour of factories, speaking to mass meetings of factory workers and generally talking about the war in the Middle East and Italy, and the RAF in particular. Frankly, the prospect alarmed me considerably. I have always disliked standing on my feet addressing a mass of people, and the thought of having to make a number of speeches for a month on end was appalling. My reaction to the suggestion must have been fairly definite; and another job was found for me just in time.

This was to command temporarily a communication flight at Inverness. The flight serviced Wick, the Orkneys and the Shetlands; and used Rapides, Oxfords and Proctors. I left Euston for Scotland at the beginning of December and spent three very cold weeks at Inverness before returning to Tonbridge for Christmas.

Apart from the cold, it was a pleasant enough period; though I remember one air test as a passenger in an Oxford which was more than usually worrying. Ice formed rapidly on the wings, and prevented any sort of climb after take-off. The result was that we weaved in between chimneys and spires of Inverness town, just above stalling speed; we were very relieved to get down again safely all in one piece. Another flight was to deliver passengers to the Orkneys; the vacant seats on the return to Inverness I filled with turkeys. Christmas was coming.

For the first stage of the journey to London I flew an Oxford to Perth. We could not get over the hills, but had to turn back and go around the coast, noticing that there was extreme vibration in the port engine. When we landed we found that the tip of the port airscrew was missing. I was glad to get aboard the train and into a sleeper. Scotland is not the best place for flying during the winter.

Christmas spent at home for the first time for three years was wonderful; and so was the prospect of starting at Hawker's. Determined to arrive at Langley in good fettle on New Year's Day, 1945 I decided to avoid all New Year's Eve celebrations. I packed up my things at Tonbridge and went over to stay at the Plough Inn, near Langley, spending a very quiet and sober evening by myself. As it turned out, this was hardly necessary, as nobody expected me to arrive before lunchtime; but I was glad to have a clear head next morning when I met Philip Lucas. He gave me a warm welcome, and a short talk about the difference between life in the RAF and a civilian factory.

"Remember," he said, "the people here are not in uniform. You'll get the best results not by giving orders but by working in with them."

I can't say that I had any intention of giving orders; and from the start I found everybody most helpful and easy and pleasant to work with. It was to be an interesting year; a year, in fact, which although I did not realize it at the time was ultimately to decide my future.

It began at a servicing school run by Hawker's. I had to learn as much as possible about the Tempest 2 and 5, to get a working knowledge of these aircraft and their engines. I found that there were two branches of test pilots at Hawker's; the production and the experimental test pilots. The chief production test pilot was Hubert Broad, one of my boyhood heroes. It was a great moment to meet him for the first time. He was then nearing fifty; he had been flying since about 1914, he had been one of the pre-war Schneider Cup team, and, before coming to Hawker's, chief test pilot at De Havilland's. The other production pilots were: Frankie Fox, who later gave up flying to go on the stage; Merrick Hymans, who had been an instructor while I was at White Waltham during my elementary flying training for the RAF, and who later took up horse-breeding; "Chips" Carpenter, DFC and Bar, whom I had known in Italy when he commanded 72 Squadron in 324 Wing; and Frankie Silk, DFC, who had flown Spitfires with a Photo Reconnaissance Unit, both of whom are still in the Air Force.

Philip Lucas was head of the experimental team; and with him were Bill Humble, and Frank Murphy, a New Zealander who had flown with a New Zealand Typhoon Squadron and had been awarded the DFC. Frank Murphy worked both on the experimental and production sides.

At that time the Hawker prototype being developed was the Fury, later to go into service with the Royal Navy in large numbers. There were three versions of the Fury, one with the Centaurus engine, another with the Sabre 7 engine, and the third with the Griffin and contra-rotating airscrews.

Hawker's had their problems in the early days of developing this aircraft, and both Lucas and Humble had to force-land. Lucas brought down a Fury safely when its fuselage fractured; he might have baled out, but he got it down, wheels up, so that the trouble might be located and corrected, and was awarded the George Medal for a very gallant effort.

I soon settled into the swing of production testing. It included: testing the aircraft and engine on the ground, checking the engine performance and temperatures and pressures in climbs, checking fuel consumption, seeing that the hydraulic system functioned properly; and noting engine boosts and revolutions; checking times to heights; and doing level speed measurements, and dives to maximum speed.

We flew every day, whenever the weather would allow, ironing out any snags that might show themselves in the aircraft, with the necessary adjustments being made by the ground staff. They worked in the flight shed and included some wonderful men who did a great job during the war—and in fact do a great job at all times.

There was Pete Lemon, the shed foreman, who usually seemed a little harassed at the end of each month if the production schedule got a bit behind; there was Charlie Ayres, who is still at Langley; and Bert Hayward, who has been with Hawker's for thirty-two years, and who now has a big hand in looking after the Hawker Hunter.

When we were satisfied that Tempests were ready for delivery, and had been passed for squadron use, they were collected at Langley by pilots of the Air Transport Auxiliary, many of them girls who flew the aircraft off with all the assurance in the world.

While working at Langley, I lived with four other test pilots at Shooters Lodge, a lovely old house at Winkfield Row, near Ascot. It was owned by Mrs Legros, and with Seth Smith, Chips Carpenter and Frankie Silk, I was a paying guest. Seth Smith was with the Fairey Aviation Co, which was then operating from a grass aerodrome which is now London Airport. Unfortunately, he was later killed when a canopy blew off a Firefly he was testing.

We had a pleasant life at Shooters Lodge, which somehow became known as "Line Shooters' Lodge". I had bought a Riley "Imp" sports car for transport between there and Langley. We got to know the owner of the nearby pub, "The Squirrel"; he was Walter Sayer, author of many books, including Sexton Blakes.

One day early in February I went up to London to attend an investiture at Buckingham Palace. My father and mother came with me, and when we got inside with what seemed to be hundreds of people, I went off to join the others who were collecting decorations.

We were sorted out into grades of decorations and seemed to queue up for hours, shuffling along after the new knights and other people who had won distinctive decorations. While a string orchestra played . . . and played . . . we moved slowly forward in the low-ceilinged Grand Hall, of which my main impressions are cream and plush colouring, and of oil paintings on the walls. Suddenly, it seemed, it was my turn to approach the King. He was in full naval uniform, and after he had pinned on the medals he enquired how long it had taken me to win them.

This ceremony came fairly soon after my twenty-third birthday; and leaving the Palace with my father and mother, we met up with Peggy and had a pleasant family party.

As the months went by and the war ended with VE and VJ celebrations—I seem to remember being in parties that lasted two days each time—I became increasingly interested in testing aircraft, and particularly experimental testing. It must have been about June that I was given a first opportunity of flying the Fury; and this was flying with a difference.

I found there was a definite taste of exploration about taking up an aircraft to discover what it would do in particular tests. I began to appreciate the greater freedom of civilian life with an aircraft manufacturing firm in which flying is a daily job.

It was during my year with Hawker's that I met Gwen—my wife—

for the first time. I was introduced to "Miss Gwendoline Fellows" in Windsor, and I was to find myself thinking a lot of Gwen, dark, petite, and very attractive. But for a long time we did not talk much.

Gwen tells me these days that whenever there was a gathering in the "South Western" in Windsor, or at "The Stag", in Datchet, she had very little opportunity of talking with me for I was usually pretty silent, listening to other people. This may have been true; all the same I knew she was there and, if perhaps I did not talk much it was good just to be there in her company. She had, I discovered, a mutual interest in aeroplanes and cars.

Occasionally, I used to see Sidney Camm, chief designer for Hawker's, who was also to take a big part in my life in later days; but I think the first time that I ever spoke to him was a year or more later while I was at the RAF Experimental Station at Boscombe Down, in Wiltshire.

I did meet, however, another of my boyhood heroes, Sir Thomas Sopwith, a grand old man of aviation, who had designed Pups and Camels during the First World War, and who started the firm which was later to take the name of Hawker in memory of Harry Hawker, a great test pilot who lost his life while flying.

Sir Thomas Sopwith is now chairman of the Hawker Siddeley group, and one of his favourite pastimes is salmon fishing. He used to arrive at Langley with a number of salmon he had caught in Scotland, and we would fly him round to the various firms in the group on what we used to call the fish run.

Sopwith often used to startle a navigator, for he has been flying round England for so many years that he seems to know his way without maps. From time to time while you were flying with him he would say something like:

"That's —— town. In ten minutes we shall be over old So-and-so's house. We had a wonderful party there in 1922." It was quite an experience to fly with him and very good for one's navigation.

During the summer of 1945 I had my first holiday in England since schooldays. Frankie Silk flew me down to the Scilly Isles in a Vega Gull, and I spent a fortnight pleasantly by myself, swimming and tramping around the islands all alone, and thinking of the future.

I had been much interested to meet Richard Muspratt, who joined Hawker's after taking a test pilot's course at Boscombe Down. When I told him of my growing interest in experimental testing, he and Bill Humble, who helped me a great deal, suggested that I should think of applying to take the Empire Test Pilot's School course, and he encouraged me to brush up my maths and to study his notes taken on the course.

I brooded over this idea during my holiday; and also acquired a spaniel puppy while on a visit to Tresco. He was a nice little chap, but he was not too keen on his first flight in the Rapide back to St Just. Later on Tresco—I called him after his birthplace—seemed to like flying and I used to take him round a lot. He died later of distemper.

During August, while I was thinking about the future, the Air Ministry offered me a permanent commission in the RAF. I had no hesitation in accepting it; and it had much to do with my applying to take the Empire Test Pilot's School course.

I was elated one morning, to receive a letter telling me to report to the Ministry of Supply headquarters in London and to appear before a Selection Board. Its members asked me a number of questions, such as why I wanted to take the course, and sounded my knowledge of flying in various directions.

Apparently I made the appropriate answers for eventually I was notified that my application had been accepted and that I was to take the Test Pilot's course after completing my year with Hawker's.

I had enjoyed my work at Langley and gained some very valuable experience; and when the time came to make my several farewells I was very proud when the personnel of the production flight shed, including Pete Lemon and Charlie Ayres, presented me with a tankard.

Soon after my twenty-fourth birthday, I joined No. 4 Course of the ETPS. I learned much at the school and the knowledge gained there gave me a solid background, enabling me to take up experimental test piloting as a career.

The school has been described as "The University of Flying". A unit of the Ministry of Supply, it is controlled administratively by a group of the Maintenance Command of the RAF, and was established in 1943 at Boscombe Down "to provide suitably trained pilots for test flying duties in the Aeronautical Research and Development Establishments within the Services and industry", being first known as "The Test Pilots' School". It is open to the RAF and the Fleet Air Arm, to civilians testing for British firms, to men from Allied Air Forces, and to those from the

Dominions' Air Forces. In 1944 it was renamed the Empire Test Pilots' School, and in October 1945 it was moved from Boscombe Down to Cranfield; in 1947 it went to Farnborough.

As the war continued and aircraft were designed and powered to fly faster and faster, test pilots were needed in increasing numbers for both production and experimental testing. They began to be regarded as specialists.

The school is directed by a commandant, and in 1946 this post was held by Group Captain H J Wilson, CBE, AFC, who established a new world speed record for Britain in 1945 by flying a Meteor at six hundred and six miles an hour. His chief test flying instructor was Wing Commander Sandy Powell, AFC, a pilot of wide experience who had flown at Martlesham Heath, Boscombe Down and Farnborough.

There were thirty-five pilots in No. 4 Course, and they included several from the RAF and the Fleet Air Arm, as well as Americans, Australians, and Chinese. One of them has since become a great friend, Wing Commander "Dickie" Martin, DFC, AFC, who flew with No. 73 Squadron in France during the early days of the war where he became for a while, "the prisoner of Luxembourg" after being shot down.

Our first three months were spent analysing the performance of a variety of aircraft, and flying anything from light trainers to jet fighters and twin-engined and four-engined bombers. The main purpose was to teach us to become critics of an aircraft and to be able to sum up its qualities merely by handling and flying it. We took many lectures: on mathematics, physics, aerodynamics, turbo-jet engine performance, the special problems of high speed and high altitude flight, current trends in research, and the physiological aspects of test flying.

We wrote long reports and, in addition to monthly tests, finished up by sitting for examinations. About a month was spent at the Royal Aircraft Establishment at Farnborough, studying the work of this important unit in wind tunnels, aircraft structure, rockets and aero-dynamics. The first part of the course lasted six months, when we broke up for a period of four months.

One of my vivid memories of Cranfield is of flying a jet for the first time. Until now all my flying had been done in piston-engined aircraft and I was very keen—and not a little curious—to fly a jet. It was a Meteor 3 and we were not given dual instruction, the present practice. We were told and shown how the aircraft worked—and off we went.

I was interested to find many differences between flying a jet and a piston-engined aircraft. To begin with the biggest difference, I suppose, is the absence of vibration in a jet; instead of an airscrew whirring round, shaking everything, the jet engines work smoothly by sucking in air.

I also noticed there is much less noise in the cockpit; but that the Meteor is slower in responding to the throttle movement than, say, a Spitfire, particularly on the approach to land. This quicker response of a Spitfire is because the airscrew bites into the air as you move the throttle. The speed of a piston-engined aircraft depends on the revolutions per minute of the airscrew; the speed of a jet depends for its power on the air flowing through its engines. A jet is more sluggish on acceleration or deceleration; but the faster it goes, the more power its engines develop.

I also found that a Meteor, for example, is easier to fly in many ways than a Spitfire. With the Spitfire, you always had the long nose of the engine stretching out in front of you, and your range of vision was partially restricted. You get a much better view sitting right in the nose of a Meteor.

There is no swing while taking off in a jet. A piston aircraft tends to swing to the left or the right, according to the direction in which the airscrew, or airscrews, are rotating. Another point is that there is no need to worry about mixture controls to regulate fuel consumption; there is just one throttle to each engine to be moved backwards or forwards.

In some way, however, a jet is a more complicated thing to fly. Fuel consumption is much greater and to get a low fuel consumption you have to fly high, since a jet becomes more economical on fuel the higher it is flown.

It is also a little more difficult to fly while making a landing approach. Being very clean-designed and with much less "drag", rather more time is required to allow speed to fall away; the result is that if you come in to land a little too fast, there is a tendency for the aircraft to "float" or to overshoot.

It was while flying a Meteor at Cranfield that I had my first experience of Mach characteristics. In a Meteor you can climb fairly high, and reach about Mach 0.8. I began to experience compressibility effects for the first time in the form of airframe buffet, changes in trim—the nose going up or down, or a wing going down—and finding that the

24.

With Gwen outside Buckingham Palace in 1945.

25.,

Members of the High Speed Flight, 1946. Neville Duke,
Bill Waterton and Teddy Donaldson. RAF Tangmere.

26.

Meteor flying low over Tangmere.

27.,

A Hawker Fury flown to Egypt.

controls became much heavier. On these occasions I used the air brakes to slow down, for just to throttle back would not reduce speed quickly enough.

As part of the course we flew Vampires as well as Meteors; and also four-engined Lancasters and Lincolns, a Hamilcar glider towed behind a Halifax bomber, a Grunau glider; and Mosquitoes, Seafires, Tempests, Dakotas and many other types. I preferred the jets to everything else, and I became increasingly interested in the problems of high speed flight.

We talked about them at the school, and I remember also discussing them with Hunk Humphreys, now back from the Middle East and commanding officer of the RAF Station at Castle Bromwich. Hunk used to give occasional parties at his station, I invited Gwen to one of these— the first time I had ever asked her out.

She tells me now that my invitation was a little odd; that I said, "I have never taken a girl to a mess dance before because it interferes with the drinking. But I know I don't have to worry about you!"

Anyway, I drove down to Maidenhead from Cranfield in a battered old car and collected her. It was a pretty good party.

Later, Gwen also came along with me to a dance at the headquarters of No. 11 Group of Fighter Command. I was so pleased to have her with me and so keen to entertain her that I put up a minor black—at least I hope it was regarded as a minor one!

There was a table laden with good things and reserved for VIP's. In my keenness to look after her appropriately I led her up to this table not realizing it was reserved. It was not quite the best way for a flight lieutenant to behave in the presence of exalted superiors. If there were any frowns, I noticed only Gwen's smiles!

About the end of June 1946 while we were finishing the first half of the test pilots' course, I was delighted when Group Captain Wilson told me that I was to be a member of the High Speed Flight to be formed at Tangmere to make another attempt on the world's speed record.

The flight was to be commanded by Group Captain Teddy Donaldson, DSO, AFC, Squadron Leader Bill Waterton, AFC, a Canadian, was to be the other pilot. The course was roughly between Bognor and Shoreham, and the record was to be attempted over a stretch of three kilometres, just opposite Littlehampton. It was a great honour to be selected, and I could think of no better way of spending my time during the interval in the test pilots' course.

I had some other good news. Gwen told me that she and a great friend, Peggy Fraser (now married to Graham Cox) were going to take a cottage at Itchenor, not far from Tangmere, for a month.

All this flying and seeing Gwen, too! I went off to Tangmere in the best of spirits.

## CHAPTER 9

# Speed—and Decisions

IN many ways, the results of Donaldson's High Speed Flight were disappointing. It is true that Donaldson increased the world's record by ten miles an hour, with a figure of 616 miles per hour, or Mach 0.81 but we had hoped to do much better. One of the main reasons was that the weather was against us. We wanted a hot sunny day, a high tide and no bumps. We got the worst summer in England for several years and plenty of bumps; when Donaldson put up the new record, the weather was cold, the sky was overcast and light rain was falling. I was not even to be present; I was in Brussels.

If there was a rather negative side to the work of this High Speed Flight, there was also a positive result too: the conventional type of aircraft form was shown to have reached the limit of its development for flying at speed. In the past the problem had been to provide an engine to fly an aircraft at high speed; from 1946 onwards it was accepted that, with the development of the turbo-jet engine, the problem would be to design an aircraft to make the fullest use of the greater engine power now available. In other words, while at Tangmere the flight could, and did occasionally, fly at 626 miles per hour, the limit of the Meteor had been reached. The era of swept-back wings and delta wings was approaching.

Tremendous organization went into the preparation for making the new record. The course had to be marked out with balloons and buoys—some two hundred buoys were used, tons of apparatus, and four mooring vessels. The length of the course was 72 kilometres or 45 miles. The record attempts had to be made under the regulations of the Fédération Aéronautique Internationale, and they included the stipulation that the aircraft were not to fly above 75 metres or 246 feet during the timed run over three kilometres, or during the 500 metres immediately preceding the timed run. Two photographic methods were used for measuring the speed of the aircraft.

"Bags of low flying," said Bill Waterton.

Throughout July and August we flew round the course in new Meteor 4's. I went round it about one hundred and eighty times. During these training flights we worked up speeds of about 595 miles per hour or about Mach Number 0.8 and we had a number of bumpy rides. These bumps could be caused either by the weather or, if the tide was out, from heat waves or thermals rising from the rocks and sand under the heat of the sun. At times you felt as though you were sitting at the top of a flight of stairs with your legs stuck out straight in front of you; and then somebody grasped your legs and pulled you all the way downstairs.

This was rather uncomfortable, and so was the occasion when one of the Rolls Royce Derwent engines failed. I was flying along at between 120 and 150 feet at some 580 miles per hour when the revolutions of the port engine fell, with the result that the aircraft swung and rolled sharply to one side; and, with the controls heavy while flying at speed, it needed some effort to keep the machine straight. I was able to cut out the port engine altogether and to fly back on the other.

One of our bogeys was the shortage of fuel capacity or to run short of fuel at any part of the course; we felt, however, that even if this did occur with the Meteors flying at round about 600 miles per hour, we should have sufficient speed to glide back to Tangmere with both engines dead. To check this theory we cut both throttles back while flying at high speed on the run down the course away from Tangmere, and found that we did have enough speed to glide back.

Towards the end of August two new Meteors were delivered for the record attempt. They had no wireless equipment, no radio mast, and no armament; extra fuel was carried in three tanks to cope with the high fuel consumption. Each also had a special cockpit hood reinforced with metal; this was in case air passing over the windscreen at high speed should heat and soften the perspex, causing bad distortion and possibly failure. When an aircraft is flying at between speeds of 600 and 640 miles per hour a rise in temperature, due to friction of the air, of between 35 to 40 degrees Centigrade can be expected.

The bad weather continued, but Donaldson reached a true air speed of 626 miles per hour during one three minute level speed test at 3,000 feet in cold, unfavourable conditions. I also remember that day, for Air

Marshal Sir James Robb, who was then AOC Fighter Command, decided that Donaldson and Waterton should make the official attempts on the record, and that I should remain as reserve pilot. I was naturally disappointed but the decision had to be taken.

Donaldson was among the RAF's leading pilots. He had been one of the pre-war aerobatic Fury team which won a competition at Zurich. He excelled at air gunnery and his marksmanship was most valuable when he led a Hurricane squadron during the early days of the war. He is a most cheerful, noisy personality. Bill Waterton had a distinguished record on fighters during the war and had aided the development of fighter tactics at the Central Fighter Establishment. Steady, con-scientious, he is a first-class pilot and is now chief test pilot for Gloster Aircraft.

I did get an opportunity to raise the record. One day Donaldson said: "When Bill comes down, jump in and have a go yourself."

After Bill had landed I waited for about half an hour while the Meteor was refuelled and a few rivets were checked.

I made several flights round the course and managed to work up 625 miles per hour for one run. I started the runs at 1,000 feet over Worthing and put the nose of the aircraft down to reach 120 feet before beginning the measured section of the course. When I opened the throttle I could feel the seat pushing into my back. The needle of the air speed indicator swung quickly over to 550 miles per hour, and then seemed to creep to 600 miles per hour. The cockpit got hotter and hotter due to the friction of the air on the hood and I began to perspire freely. Compressibility developed and I found the aircraft beginning to shudder and vibrate quite violently; the nose began to drop and the port wing to dip. I had to use both hands firmly on the control column and to prop my left shoulder against the side of the cockpit to help keep the Meteor straight on the course.

Looking out, I could see the line of marker buoys flashing past almost like a blur, while an air-sea rescue flying boat on patrol out at sea appeared to be standing still. The marked vibration or buffet continued until, on passing beyond the buoys marking the end of the measured three kilometres, I eased back the throttles. The nose and the wing came up and I was able to fly with one hand again. My main impressions of the flight were of terrific noise from the air rushing past the fuselage and from the engines; of the sudden increase of heat in the cockpit; and of a feeling of exhilaration at flying so fast so near the sea. My average speed was 614 miles per hour.

When Donaldson put up the new record the temperature was 14 degrees Centigrade—we had hoped for 30 degrees—and rain drops were falling although it was not raining hard. Conditions were bumpy, and when Bill Waterton made his runs, the first was a wash-out after he struck a bad bump at the start which threw him off course. He did an extra run to make up for this and his times were only slightly lower than Donaldson's.

As I have mentioned, I was to be in Brussels when Donaldson broke the record. I flew to Melsbroek, just outside Brussels, and from there took-off during the following day, a Saturday, to show the Meteor's paces at an international air rally at Ghent. I gave an aerobatic display, which seemed to go down fairly well, for the Meteor was then a comparatively new and rare machine, particularly overseas. After the display the Burgomaster of Ghent gave a banquet and, following Continental custom, presented those who had taken part with a bronze plaque.

Not long afterwards, there was an air display at Prague, and I was detailed to take the Meteor there. The flight was made in stages, with stops at Melsbroek, Wiesbaden and Furth, near Nuremburg. A Lincoln bomber carried the ground crew for the Meteor and the team was headed by Wing Commander Bell. Before landing at Furth I had a look at the stadium in Nuremburg where the Nazis used to hold their big party rallies. When I landed, swarms of American GI's came round the Meteor; they had not seen one before.

I took off from Furth for Prague about dusk, and after flying in the dark for fifteen minutes the city appeared on time. I spent a little while admiring the lights before landing. The Czechs were very keen for the Meteor to arrive the day before the show which decided me to risk the night flight over strange territory. Our's was not the only jet there. The Americans had three F 80's, but when the display began two of them would not start, the pilot hopped from one to the other and managed to get off in the third, though he had to force-land shortly afterwards.

My two smiling and happy airmen did an excellent job on the Meteor, and we had no snags. I was able to put the aircraft through all its paces and the Czech people, who had not seen a Meteor flying before, became enthusiastic.

Indeed they were rather too enthusiastic. When I had landed I realized that swarms of people were running towards the aircraft from all directions. The crowd had broken the barriers surrounding the airfield, and in their keenness to have a closer look at the machine they were soon massed thickly round. I learned afterwards that about 150,000 people were there.

It was an alarming experience—alarming because of the danger they ran from the jet engines. Those who might get too close to the intakes could easily be sucked into the engine, and those who came too near the exhausts could be burned. In the end, I had to stop taxiing and cut the engines. Then I had to sit there, grinning and feeling rather foolish, as the crowd milled around the aircraft, touching it and pushing and pulling the ailerons. While I was wondering what came next, one of the airmen appeared, and helped me from the cockpit. When I was out, he sat in it to lash up the controls; and when I was finally rescued by some police and escorted away I looked back to see him trapped in the cockpit, being mistaken for the pilot. He had pulled the canopy over him and was sitting crouched there looking rather despondent. I don't know how long he had to remain.

The Czechs were just as enthusiastic in their hospitality as they had been over the Meteor. We had some wonderful parties that evening, and I was rather pleased though also embarrassed, when I was decorated with the Czech Military Cross.

Air Marshal Sir John Boothman, CB, the famous and popular Schneider Trophy pilot of the early thirties who retained the trophy for Britain, had also flown over to Prague for the display in his photographic reconnaissance Spitfire. He had been closely connected with the High Speed Flight and his advice and experience had been of great value. He was also decorated by the Czechs and so was the pilot of the Lincoln, who impressed everybody by making a fly-past on one engine.

We were due to take off the following morning after dawn on the return to Melsbroek, but a heavy mist delayed our leaving with the result that breakfast almost became another party. All sorts of people joined in, and some Russians who showed curiosity in the Meteor stood around staring at it for a time, and then disappeared.

After a number of explanations that cognac was not usual for breakfast in England, I was able to take off. The plan had been for me to land at Wiesbaden and to meet up there again with the Lincoln and the ground crew. But the weather was so fine and clear when I left Prague and visibility so good that I decided to push on straight to Melsbroek. As it turned out this was an unwise decision, for the weather clamped down as I neared Brussels. I had to fly around trying to find Melsbroek, with an anxious eye on the fuel gauge. It had been a long flight and eventually, to save fuel, I cut one engine and flew on the other. In the end I force-landed at Beauvachaine, near Brussels, but found no facilities for refuelling the Meteor. The Belgians drove me into Brussels, located the Shell Company and got them to fix up the aircraft.

Meanwhile, there was a concern at Wiesbaden among the Lincoln boys. I had been unable to contact them by radio, but had relied on getting in touch with them from Melsbroek, and as I had not landed at Wiesbaden they imagined that I must be missing. In the end we all met safely at Melsbroek, stayed the night in Brussels, and flew back to Tangmere via Manston the following day. There we made one or two more efforts to improve on Donaldson's record, but we were unable to reach a higher average figure for four runs. Air Marshal Sir James Robb finally ordered that no further attempts were to be made. Ironically it seemed, the day following this order was the best of the summer, clear, hot, bright—just what we wanted. But Sir James would not reverse his order, and no doubt it was a wise decision. That same day Geoffrey de Havilland, who was to have made an attack any day on Donaldson's record, was killed in the DH 108. It was a sad loss.

And so the flight broke up. It had been a great experience for the three of us, and in addition, provided valuable information for the RAF and the aircraft manufacturers about the effects of flying at high speed at a very low altitude.

I had enjoyed Tangmere a great deal, and not only because of the flying. It had been wonderful to have Gwen so near at Itchenor with Peggy. Their cottage, old and characterful, was a general meeting place, and Hunk and Graham Cox came down several times. We spent many pleasant and happy hours together; but the blow came when Gwen and Peggy returned to Maidenhead. I felt very lonely without Gwen, as lost as when I left home for the first time. I soon realized that I wanted to ask her to marry me.

In the meantime, however, there was the second half of the test pilots' course to be completed at Cranfield and I returned to carry on with the good work and to pass, receiving the school's diploma. This stated that I was a graduate of the Empire Test Pilots' School, and had satisfactorily completed all flying and technical exercises of the course "in the performance testing and handling of all representative classes of landplanes in present use and satisfied the examiners at the end of the course".

After Cranfield, I was to go to the Aeroplane and Armament Experimental Establishment at Boscombe Down, the Ministry of Supply's testing ground for all aircraft before they go into Service use.

Gwen and I had now decided to get married. It was impossible to obtain a house near Boscombe, but we were offered a small cottage at Bray, near Maidenhead. Although this meant a certain amount of separation, it would be preferable to digs closer at hand.

But first I wanted to tell my father and mother the news. I went over to Tonbridge for Christmas; neither my parents nor Peggy had met Gwen so they were naturally a little startled when I said, rather abruptly perhaps:

"I'm going to get married!"

Father, mother and Peggy put down their knives and forks and stared at me in silence—an embarrassing moment.

Then father said:

"Well, my boy, if you think it's all right, we will too."

The following weekend I collected Gwen in the car, took her to Tonbridge, and we all had a very happy afternoon tea; and I was delighted to find that the family and Gwen got on well together. I knew they would.

We were married by the Reverend Adcock the following March on the 15th—in the twelfth century church at Dorney, near Windsor. But not without complications. The winter of 1946–7 was one of the worst in recent memory, snow lying on the ground for weeks. And just before we were to be married the thaw set in, flooding the Thames Valley for miles around.

Parts of Maidenhead were well under water, and Gwen's house was hemmed in by floods. She had to be carried, in all her finery, to a dinghy and be rowed to dry land before setting off for the church. Everything went off as it should, Hunk was in good form and we had a grand party at the reception for which Derek Livesey, the best man, and his wife, loaned their house at Dorney.

But the floods were to cause further complications. We had planned to stay at the "Hind's Head" at Bray and to fly to Brussels the following day for our honeymoon. While we were driving from Dorney to Bray, I in my MG and Gwen in her Hillman, we ran into flood water eighteen inches deep. The Hillman stalled and I had to get out in my best blues, and with the flood water swirling around my thighs, fix a rope to tow Gwen. The water was very cold and very muddy and I must have looked a bedraggled groom arriving at the "Hind's Head".

Back from Brussels we settled in to Green Shutters, next door to the "Hind's Head" at Bray. I was now at Boscombe Down. I left there in my car every Friday for home and returned at 6 a.m. again on the Monday. It seemed the best way of working things out for the time being.

At Boscombe I was posted to the Fighter Test Squadron commanded by Wing Commander John Baldwin, DSO, DFC, AFC, who was later to be reported missing in Korea. Boscombe has been the centre of test flying for many years, and, among other things, it is there that acceptance trials of new aircraft—or prototype aircraft—are carried out before they go into service with the RAF or the Fleet Air Arm. We worked on Meteors, Vampires, Hornets, Mosquitos, Spitfires, Tempests and various trainers.

The experience I had gained with the High Speed Flight now proved most useful, and I was directed to carry out research work with Meteors at high Mach numbers and high altitudes. Not to be too technical, this meant taking a Meteor up to 40-50,000 feet, putting it through tests and recording the speed at which the aircraft began to buffet or to shudder as compressibility effects developed, and noting the changes in trim and the forces required to hold these effects. Some of the tests required straight stalls, stalls in turns or under G, up to the highest possible altitudes. This was to determine the aircraft's limits of manoeuvrability and the effects of Mach number on it under these conditions. These tests eventually gave a complete picture of the manoeuvrability, speed and handling characteristics of an aircraft at heights up to its maximum ceiling.

The months ticked by, and I enjoyed life thoroughly at Boscombe. I knew now that experimental testing interested me far more than any other type of peacetime flying, but, quite naturally, I wondered what the Air Ministry would do with me when the period of my posting at Boscombe ended. It was too much to hope that I could continue flying;

there are too many other branches in the RAF for a regular officer to take part in, such as administration and staffwork, to allow him to go on flying indefinitely. The prospect of giving up flying was not altogether pleasing. With my initial training, operational tours, periods of instruction, the test pilots' course, the High Speed Flight and now Boscombe Down, I had been flying continually for eight years, including three-and-a-half years' testing: far from being tired of it, I wanted to go on.

Gwen fully realized this, and she did her best to help me. As it turned out, it was a very good best.

A near neighbour at Bray was Bill Humble, now chief test pilot at Hawker's, having succeeded Philip Lucas. I mentioned to Bill, on several occasions, my keenness to continue experimental testing, and he said that he would like to see me in the Hawker team.

One day, when I happened to land at Langley, Bill asked me if I would like to join Hawker's, giving up the RAF as a career. He said that he intended to stop flying shortly, and that he hoped Wimpy Wade would be appointed chief test pilot, and that I would become Wimpy's No. 2.

Now that the opportunity for me to continue as an experimental test pilot had arrived, the more I began to think about it, the harder I found it to make a decision.

Gwen, quite rightly, was firm on one point: the decision would have to be mine entirely.

"I shall be quite happy whatever you do. But you must make up your mind yourself," she said.

I began to sound out a few opinions at Boscombe. They were against my giving up the RAF as a career. Various people pointed out that I was now a squadron leader again at the age of twenty-six, and that with my background, there should be a good future for me in the service with a pension at the end of it. It was true that I might not get as much flying, but then they said, sooner or later, most people in the RAF tended to fly less as they climbed in rank.

While the arguments for and against were going on in my mind, I found that I should have to decide fairly quickly. Air Commodore Pelly, the Commandant at Boscombe, told me one day that I was to go to the United States to be fitted out with the latest type of pressure suit for high altitude tests. I felt that I could not accept the visit to America, and then return to say I intended to leave the RAF. I had to make a decision.

I made it one afternoon while driving back to Bray from Boscombe Down. It was a beautifully clear, sunny day, and I took a short cut over Salisbury Plain. I pulled up the car near Kingsclere and just sat there, looking at the broad expanse of countryside, green, attractive, bathed in yellow light; the sky mottled with great galleons of cumulus cloud.

I weighed up the pros and cons. I liked the life in the Air Force; enjoyed the comradeship and the service flying; it was a good career and, so far, I had not blotted my copybook. There seemed a future and an assured income when I retired. In civil testing there was no guaranteed future. But somehow experimental flying seemed to be so much more worthwhile in peacetime than anything else I could think of. There was greater freedom to be found working with a civilian firm; and what could be better than taking a hand in helping to develop the new and most interesting types of aircraft that were coming along during the next few years.

I sat looking at the countryside, pondering. But I knew what I really wanted to do, I think, before I stopped the car. I wanted to join Hawker's. I decided to accept Bill Humble's offer.

Gwen was very understanding when I told her on my arrival home.

"The main thing," she said, "is to be happy and contented with what you are doing, and you will only be that while you are flying.

Then I had to face an awkward few minutes with Air Commodore Pelly.

I went to see him when I got back to Boscombe on the Monday and he began immediately talking about my prospective trip to America.

Eventually I managed to stumble out:

"I'm sorry, sir, but I shall not be going to America. I'm requesting to resign my Commission to take a position with Hawker's as an experimental test pilot."

The Air Commodore was silent for a few moments.

Then he said:

"Well, Neville, I'm sorry—for personal reasons—to think that you will be leaving the Air Force. But if that's what you want to do, well I wish you all the best of luck."

It was an awkward moment for me, and I have never forgotten the Air Commodore's kindness and understanding.

So my decision was completed. I was glad it was over, and, although there were moments when, inevitably I suppose, I wondered whether I had done the right thing, I always came back to the comfortable feeling that now I would be able to go on flying and to do the type of work that interested me more than anything else.

CHAPTER 10

# *Civil Life*

WHEN I left the RAF in June 1948, eight years had passed since I had reported at Uxbridge to appear before a selection board. They had been eight wonderful years. I had enjoyed life. I had made firm friendships. But many friends had been killed on operations and in accidents. They included Hunk Humphreys.

While I was still at Boscombe Down and in the Air Force, Hunk had spent a week's leave with Gwen and myself at Bray. We had enjoyed the days together and looked back, perhaps a little nostalgically, to Biggin and the desert and Italy. Then he had gone off to the headquarters of No. 12 Group of Fighter Command at Nottingham.

"Staff job now," he said. "See you soon."

But we never saw him again. He went as a passenger in a Lincoln bomber during fighter affiliation exercises to observe mock attacks made by the fighters. A Hornet, making a head-on attack, misjudged the break-away and collided with the Lincoln. All in the bomber were killed and also the Hornet's pilot. Gwen and I felt Hunk's death very much; it seemed so pointless that he should be killed in such a way after coming safely through so many wartime operations.

In the period between my leaving the RAF and joining Hawker's, Gwen and I decided to take a holiday and to go south for sunshine. We set off for the south of France in my 1932 MG two-seater.

"You'll never get there in that ancient thing," some of our friends told us. "And even if you do get there, you'll never get back."

But we made the trip to Le Lavandou, both ways, without any hitches, being six days on the road altogether. For eight days we basked on Riviera beaches and bathed and collected impressive sun tans. On several occasions I tried to find the air strip we had used during the invasion of Southern France; but all trace of war had disappeared. It was a pleasant break. We returned to Bray feeling very fit.

And now, for the first time since we had been married, Gwen and I were able to make our home together. Instead of driving off to Boscombe Down at the end of each weekend I was able to travel to and from Langley each day. After years of messing, regular home life was most enjoyable, and I was able to collect many of my things round me again in a den of my own.

Although it was a new experience to report at Hawker's in August to begin civilian life, it was also something of a return home, for most of the people I had known two-and-a-half years before were still with the firm.

There had been some changes. Hubert Broad had joined Dowty's, makers of undercarriages; Muspratt had gone to Australia to sell tractors. Bill Humble was chief test pilot and Wimpy Wade, whom I had last seen when 92 Squadron was at Biggin Hill, was his No. 2. Frank Murphy was chief production test pilot, with E S ("Doc") Morrell, who had served with the Fleet Air Arm, as his No. 2. There had been few changes in the flight shed, and my old friends Pete Lemon, Charlie Ayres, and Bert Hayward were all there and gave me a warm welcome. Not long after I arrived, Bill Humble finally gave up test flying and was appointed sales manager for Hawker's. He is now the Hawker-Siddeley group representative in the Middle East with headquarters at Cyprus. Wimpy Wade moved up to chief test pilot and I became his No. 2.

We worked on Furies, Tempests and the new jet P 1040.

While I found the development of the latter most interesting I also found that adjusting myself to civilian life took a little time. After the first few weeks of initial excitement and fresh interest there followed a period of mental reaction and regret that I had left the Air Force. Looking back, I suppose this was natural for, apart from a short period, I had been in the service since leaving school. I began to miss the life and my friends, the prospect of going abroad, squadron flying and also the wide variety of aircraft to fly. I became rather restless.

This phase ended shortly after I learned that a Hawker Tomtit was for sale. The type was designed in 1928 a two-seater trainer biplane with a 130 hp Armstrong-Siddeley Mongoose engine with five cylinders, a top speed estimated at 120 miles an hour and a cruising speed of between 85 and 90 miles per hour. It had belonged to Shea Simonds, a

Supermarine test pilot, and it had been given a Spitfire windscreen and a faired headrest to the rear cockpit from which it was usually flown.

I remembered the Tomtit. One summer evening during the middle 'thirties I had seen a Tomtit doing aerobatics at West Malling. I thought then that it was the most handsome machine I had ever seen; it had open cockpits, lots of struts and bracing wires and fabric, a radial engine with plenty of oil flying around, and it seemed to be full of character.

When I began to make enquiries I found that the Tomtit was not only for sale but that it appeared to be the only one of its type left. Soon I was telling myself that if I bought it I could fly where I liked and how I liked in my spare time. Before very long I had sold my car, the MG, and become the owner of G-AFTA. It was something of a genuine antique, but it had plenty of personality which sometimes included a reluctance to start.

Doc Morrell was interested for he had a half share in a Tiger Moth, being part owner with Major T S Willans, who had once been a rodeo rider in Australia and was now a freelance test parachutist, known to everybody as "Dumbo".

"Let's team up," Doc suggested. "Let's work out an old-time dog-fight routine and take part in air displays. You can do a few aerobatics and Dumbo can do the odd drop, then we can make the two machines pay for themselves. They pay about a fiver a time for aerobatics at these displays."

Dumbo proved a good organizer, entered our aircraft in several displays, made all the necessary arrangements and then gave us a general briefing. During the summer of 1949 we flew in a number of air displays, including White Waltham, Cowes, Rearsby in Leicestershire, Beaulieu in Hampshire, and Eaton Bray. Gwen always came along in the Tomtit, thoughtfully providing sandwiches and thermos flasks of hot coffee or tea, and sometimes she sat in the front cockpit during our dog-fights.

I still have a programme billing us at Eaton Bray. It says:

"Event No. 5. Aerial dog-fight. This, the most thrilling and spectac-ular attraction in the display, will consist of a duel between the Blue Hawker Tomtit, piloted by Mr Duke, and the orange and silver Tiger Moth, piloted by Doc Morrell. Both Messrs Duke and Morrell are test pilots at the Hawker Aircraft Company, and are equally at home in high-speed military aircraft as they are in the machines they will be flying to-

28.,

With Gwen and Wimpy Wade after my return from the flight to Karachi.

29.,

With Bill Humble, Hawker's No. 2 test pilot when I joined them.

day. After gaining sufficient height, each pilot will spar for an opening to attack his opponent. The battle quickens, until finally . . . but wait and see! The climax, we think, will leave you gasping!"

In this particular display Doc also gave a demonstration of crazy-flying, and I towed F Marmol, flying a Zlin glider, to Elstree for another display.

Our "duel" with Doc was quite amusing—at least to us. While Dumbo secreted himself in the Tiger Moth, we threshed around the place making mock attacks, and just when our time was up, Doc put the Tiger Moth into a spin as Dumbo baled out and the announcer downstairs declared that the "kill" had been made.

These displays were not without their incidents. Unfortunately Dumbo was injured at Eaton Bray when he was dragged by his parachute. Gwen was not flying with me on this occasion; she ran across the field to Dumbo while I circled above, and after helping to remove his parachute harness organized his removal to hospital. A cracked collarbone put him out of action for a couple of months, and he stayed with us at Bray while recovering. Gwen and I are not likely to forget the display at Beaulieu on Battle of Britain Day in 1950. There was quite a big programme with many types of aircraft taking part—Sunderlands, Solents, Tempests, Yorks, Tiger Moths, Lincolns, helicopters, the Airspeed Ambassador, Meteors, a Swift, a Bristol Freighter and the Canadair. There were also landbattles, showing the difference between warfare in 1849 and 1949. In the 1949 battle paratroopers were landed and there was a fine old mix up. But what we did not know was that part of the airfield was strewn with mines to make the warfare more realistic.

On arrival we circled Beaulieu aerodrome, and as we came in to land we noticed rather more than usual animation among groups of soldiers who, when they saw the Tomtit about to touch down, began haring away as fast as they could go, some of them shaking a fist at us. We thought they were putting up quite a good performance for the crowd. What they were trying to do, of course, was to keep us away from the minefield. We landed slap in the middle of it in blissful ignorance, somehow avoided touching off a mine, and pulled up still wondering why the soldiers had appeared quite so excitable. We were soon told the reason in terse and vivid language, and, later on, when we saw the mines go off we did a little quiet gulping ourselves. However, the crowd enjoyed it.

As it turned out, Beaulieu was to be our final display. We stayed overnight and before leaving on the return flight to Langley made the usual check on fuel. The Tomtit's gauge showed the tank to be half full. We used 73 octane and at Beaulieu there was only 100 octane available for topping up; even with the tank half-full we had twelve gallons, more than sufficient to reach Langley.

After taking off, we hummed along steadily at about 88 miles per hour and at about 500 feet. When we were just about over Ascot I shouted to Gwen to bob down in the front cockpit so that I could see the petrol gauge for a check up. It registered one quarter full; plenty to reach home.

At that moment the motor cut dead without even a cough —we were to discover later that the gauge was faulty and the petrol tank dry. I took a hasty glance around and everywhere I looked I seemed to notice the biggest oak trees I have ever seen in my life. Then I noticed a ploughed field. It was this or nothing. I banked steeply between two trees. It was rather a tense moment. We could hear only the wind whistling a little eerily round the wires. Then we touched down, one wing went low into the earth and its tip gave a good exhibition of a plough at work.

I held the stick back hard hoping that the Tomtit would not go right over on its nose. After what seemed hours we stopped, the wing tip still covered with soil, the undercarriage bent. I was jerked forward over the stick and my head cracked against the front of the cockpit. Fortunately, Gwen was not hurt.

We felt rather self-conscious sitting there in the middle of that ploughed field, a very quiet and still field. Then suddenly men, women and children—particularly children—seemed to appear from everywhere. They ran, stumbling over the uneven earth, and soon we were surrounded by an excitable, sympathetic, curious crowd. We did not take quite such a good view of the small boys who began pulling the elevators to see how they worked.

We had landed not far from friends, near Shooters Lodge and the Crispin Inn. I examined the Tomtit and decided that I could get it off again after a bit of repair and preparation. The local police kindly kept watch during the night to guard against souvenir hunters, and next day we filled up the tank, and having made a runway by driving a car up and down and over the furrows, I was able to get the Tomtit up and away to Langley.

It was the finish of our displays, however, for though the aircraft was soon made serviceable again, Doc and Dumbo had decided to sell their Tiger Moth. It had all been good fun and experience.

My interest now turned to joining the Royal Auxiliary Air Force. I ran into Squadron Leader Peter Devitt, of Sevenoaks, who was commanding officer of 615 County of Surrey Squadron, and when he learned that I was considering the idea of becoming an auxiliary so that I could maintain my interest in and associations with the Air Force and also take part in service flying again, he told me that, reluctantly, he would have to give up his command for business reasons. He suggested that it might be possible for me to succeed him.

The thought appealed to me tremendously, particularly as the head-quarters of 615 Squadron were at Biggin Hill. Soon the necessary arrangements were made, I went to a squadron party to meet everybody, and I took over command in September 1950.

The squadron's town headquarters were in Croydon and we used to meet there every Thursday for lectures and dining-in nights. On Saturdays and Sundays we assembled at Biggin Hill for squadron training, first on Spitfire 22's and later on Meteor 4's. There we met the pilots of 600 City of London Auxiliary Squadron, commanded by Squadron Leader Jack Meadows, DFC, AFC, and worked with them. The commanding officer of the station was Wing Commander (now Group Captain) Arthur Donaldson, DSO, DFC, AFC, brother of Teddy Donaldson, who had a regular RAF squadron under his command, No. 41 as well as the two auxiliary squadrons. Arthur is a great personality and an exceptional station commander; he treated the problem of the "week-end pilots" With great understanding. He allowed them to bring their wives or girl friends to the station at certain periods during the weekends and opened the Biggin bar and mess to them. It is no small attraction to visit this famous station and we found that our attendances for squadron training began to be a byword.

615 takes great pride in its Honorary Air Commodore. He is Sir Winston Churchill, the Prime Minister, who maintains a close interest in its work and activities. Before joining 615 I had seen him twice in the distance, once when he made a visit of inspection to Biggin in 1941 and again when he accompanied the late King during His Majesty's stay in Italy in 1944.

In 1950 Sir Winston was the Leader of the Opposition and, from time to time, he used to entertain members of 615. But I was surprised, elated, and not a little nervous when our adjutant, Bob Shillingford, told me that the two of us were invited to meet the great man and to lunch with him at his country home, Chartwell, in Westerham, Kent. We both felt that it was a great honour and a privilege. It was also to prove exhilarating. We were introduced by Mr Christopher Soames, MP, a son-in-law, and Sir Winston quickly put us at ease by his friendliness, his good humour and his deep knowledge and enthusiasm for aviation. He told us something of his experiences of flying during the first world war with Major Scott, with whom he had a narrow escape when their aircraft force-landed and both were covered with petrol. Major Scott was badly injured but fortunately he managed to turn off the switches and prevent danger from fire.

While we were talking about present-day flying I happened to mention that we had been experimenting with a rocket motor in the P 1040. Sir Winston asked me a number of questions and then requested that I write him a short report on my views about rocket propulsion. He always had a great interest in the trends of future development as well as a firm knowledge of current progress in aviation.

After lunch, Sir Winston showed us over his famous house. At that time he was starting his aquarium of tropical fish, of which he had two. He showed them to us with enthusiasm, and also his study. Its walls are covered with photographs of historic events; and he has framed and hung letters from the late President Roosevelt, together with a chart of the progress of the U-boat warfare at a critical stage during the recent war. He also has a number of models, including one of the famous Mulberry Harbour. Sir Winston is obviously a lover of animals, for in addition to his fish he has a poodle, Rufus, which he insists on feeding himself. He has a cat, too, and while fondling it points out a cut it received to an ear from a splinter of glass during the blitz. Before we left he signed and presented me with a copy of his latest war memoirs—a gift to 615—and we came away much inspired by our talk with this great Englishman.

It was not to be our only visit. On another occasion he invited the officers of the squadron to Chartwell for a cocktail party after he had paid an official visit of inspection to see us at Biggin Hill when we were on a period of three months' continuous training. He took the greatest interest in our work; and we saw him twice more at Biggin—when he returned from a conference at Strasbourg, and from a Conservative

Party conference at Blackpool. On the latter occasion 615 was at readiness, with all the pilots in their Mae Wests and flying gear. They felt greatly honoured when he went round, chatting and talking.

The cocktail party at Chartwell delighted 615. Sir Winston showed us both the inside of Chartwell and also its grounds. I remember that the tropical fish had been moved upstairs, and there were now many more of them— they have since been transferred to Chequers, the move being entitled "Operation Fish". In the grounds of Chartwell we saw the famous wall which Sir Winston built himself during a period while he was in the political wilderness; the waterfalls and pools full of fish, which come to him when he calls and feeds them; his cinema and also many of his delightful oil paintings. Everybody was absorbed by his conversation and the contrasts of his facial expressions. While talking on a serious subject he looks grim and most forbidding. Suddenly an amusing thought will occur to him; his face lights up as he smiles and has an almost cherubic look. This party, enlivened with champagne cocktails, together with his short address and talk during the luncheon that followed his official visit to 615, were some of the high spots of squadron life during my period with it.

CHAPTER 11

# Records and Races

ROME was bathed in sunshine during the early morning of May 12th, 1949 and my first glimpse of the Eternal City after nearly five years was heartening. Yet I had not time for memories or sight-seeing. I had to land my Hawker Fury quickly at Ciampino airport, just outside Rome. But where was Ciampino? It was hidden by a thick rug of cloud, the only patch for miles.

I called up the control tower by radio telephone and asked for a visibility report.

A voice crackled in English:

"Visibility 300 feet. Cloud ceiling zero."

This seemed optimistic to me. Low cloud on top of thick fog covered all but the tops of trees. I flew the Fury over the area where I estimated the airport lay and asked the control tower whether they could hear my engine. They could not. I made another circuit.

My earphones crackled:

"OK. We have heard you now and recorded your time."

I was relieved but disappointed at this hitch in the plans for I was attempting to establish two records while delivering a Hawker Fury to the Royal Pakistan Air Force—from London to Rome and from London to Karachi.

The Fury has a top speed of 445 miles per hour at 19,000 feet and a cruising speed of over 400 miles per hour at 20,000 feet; its maximum range with overload tanks is about 2,000 miles. It has four 20 mm cannons and can carry rockets or two 1,000 lb bombs. It is a useful operational aircraft, pleasant to handle and ideal for long distance flying.

Several Furies were to be delivered to the RPAF at Karachi, and since there was a chance of establishing two new records, we at Hawker's felt

132

that a special effort might be made with the first delivery. John Derry had flown a Vampire 5 to Rome in 2 hours 50 minutes 40 seconds in November, 1948 and Air Marshal Sir John D'Aeth had reached Karachi with a Lancastrian Aries in 19 hours 14 minutes. I believed that the Hawker Fury could improve on both these times.

Planning the flight required much care and took a long time. We had to arrange for refuelling at Rome, Cyprus and Bahrein; we had to work out the best time for take-off from London Airport and attend to many other details including visas and inoculations. The date was partially decided by the state of the moon and to provide that most of the journey should be in daylight but that take-off from Bahrein should be in the dark.

Eventually May 10th was selected with take-off from London Airport at 3.30 a.m., forty minutes before dawn; stops of one hour each were allowed for the three refuelling points. At the last moment a minor snag developed with one of the wing tanks and, with a forecast for good weather on May 12th, the flight was delayed. During the preceding afternoon I flew the Fury from Langley to London Airport, went to bed in the early evening and got up at midnight. Gwen and Frank Murphy came along to see me off, and Bert Hayward gave me a lucky farthing and assured me that it could be useful as a disc if there should be complications with the cartridge-starter.

The London Airport runway was superbly illuminated and the Fury climbed away smoothly; and, after piercing thick cloud, I found clear starlit weather at my cruising height of 21,000 feet. It was a cold flight, especially near the Alps.

Soon I flew into high snow-storm clouds and began to climb again. At 27,500 feet there was an unpleasant moment when I noticed that the oil temperature was going right off the clock. The Bristol Centaurus engine was at some strain at this height and the high temperature was probably caused by oil tending to freeze and not circulate in the cooler. I was now flying over the middle of the Alps and, with the engine still running sweetly, I decided on the blind eye principle. From now on this gauge became unserviceable and I was probably saved some worry later in the flight while flying through the heat of the Middle East.

Northern Italy was fairly clear of cloud and soon I began to look forward to a comfortable landing at Ciampino airport; but it was blotted out. Once I heard that my time was taken for the London-Rome leg, I had to get down quickly somewhere to refuel and press on again. I remembered being based at Urbe, some 20 miles away from Ciampino, with 244 Wing during the war; so I flew off to this airfield and landed to meet with complications and frustration.

The Italians at Urbe knew nothing about my Fury, nor of my hope of new records, and were indifferent to my gesticulations which I hoped would convey to them that I wanted to get away again as soon as possible. I guessed that the Shell representatives would soon appear, and began to prepare the aircraft for refuelling. They arrived after half an hour's fast driving, bringing the petrol and also the official time-keepers; with them was Flight Sergeant Chinaworth ex-112 Squadron whom I had known in 1941 and was delighted to see again. He worked like mad to get the Fury ready.

During refuelling I learned that my time for the 908.3 miles from London was 2 hours 30 minutes 58.4 seconds, about twenty minutes faster than John Derry's in the Vampire 5.

This was cheering; but there were further complications.

The director of the Urbe airfield would not allow me to take-off. He had my passport, but he had no authority to allow me to leave.

"Ring up Ciampino."

But there had been a heavy thunderstorm the previous evening, all the telephone lines to Ciampino were down and that airfield seemed to be temporarily isolated.

"Get them on the r/t—speak to control tower there from the Fury."

"That is against all rules and regulations."

"Send somebody to the Air Ministry."

We fumed and fretted as valuable time ticked by. Eventually, and thanks to the Shell representatives, an official note came from the Italian Air Ministry authorizing my take-off. Having landed at Urbe at 7.26 a.m. I was airborne again at 9.03 a.m. but instead of this stop being confined to one hour I had been on the ground for an hour and a half. It was not until I was well on the way to Cyprus, cruising at 360 miles per hour at 21,000 feet with visibility so good that I could see for fifty miles, that my irritation began to evaporate. The Mediterranean looked clear and blue; Albania, Greece and Turkey soon slipped out of sight; the 1,220 miles to Cyprus were covered in three-and-a-quarter hours.

There were no complications at Cyprus. Wing Commander Deacon Elliott, DFC, the station commander, whom I had known in 72

Squadron at Biggin in 1941 had everything well organized. He and Wing Commander Alan Deere, DSO, DFC, the celebrated New Zealand pilot whom I had also met at Biggin, gave me a warm welcome; Cyprus Airways provided a cold lunch, and the refuelling was so efficient that I was flying again after twenty-five minutes. Everything, including the weather, seemed perfect.

However, after crossing the Syrian coast I ran into cloud up to 25,000 feet. It continued without break until I was near Habbaniya so that I had to fly on instruments and plot my position by dead reckoning—by time and speed—for I could not see the ground. Sandstorms and more cloud hid the earth after Habbaniya had been passed, but luckily I managed to arrive exactly over Kuwait and then there was a clear run down the Persian Gulf to Bahrein which I reached at dusk. As the Fury slid down from 21,000 feet to land I began to feel that I was entering an oven. The time for the 1,267 miles from Cyprus to Bahrein was 3 hours 26 minutes. Once again, the RAF and the Shell Company were immaculately efficient and I was flying again after another break for refuelling of twenty-five minutes. There was one uneasy moment when it was discovered that a gland on one of the oxygen bottles was leaking, but this was soon fixed.

By flying eastwards, I had caught up with the night again and I took off into a sky filled with thousands of stars and a huge full moon. As the Fury had no cockpit lighting it was necessary to check instruments and read maps by torchlight. I must have been getting rather tired by this time for I found myself studying the maps by torch-light and then shining the torch through the canopy to look at the Baluchistan coastline 21,000 feet below! In the moonlight it looked hostile and inhospitable, no place for a forced landing. I had been told that the sea was filled with sharks and other unfriendly fish.

But it was a pleasant flight to Karachi and, when I landed at Mauripur to be met by Air Vice-Marshal R L R Atcherley, CB, CBE, AFC, Chief of the Royal Pakistan Air Force, and many of his officers, I found that my time from London had been 15 hours 18 minutes 36 seconds. I had hoped to make it 15 hours dead; but at least the Fury had put up two new records.

These two records, London to Rome 2 hours 30 minutes 58.4 seconds, and London to Karachi 15 hours 18 minutes 36 seconds have since been beaten. John Cunningham flew the De Havilland Comet to

Rome in 1 hour 59 minutes 37 seconds on March 16th, 1950. On January 27th, 1953, when Flight Lieutenant L M Whittington and Flight Lieutenant J A Brown flew a Canberra from London to Karachi in 8 hours 52 minutes 28.2 seconds, they went on to reach Darwin just over 22 hours after leaving London, a great effort.

After two pleasant days in Karachi I flew in an RPAF Bristol Freighter to Peshawar, near the North-West Frontier, a base for fighter wings equipped with Tempest 2's, and my imagination was stirred by a glimpse of the Khyber Pass. I learned that a tribal war was still in progress with the Fakir of Ipi on the Afghanistan border and that the Tempests were being used periodically to give his troops a taste of rockets.

From Peshawar I was taken on to Risalpur in a Harvard to give a short lecture at the Flying College and a demonstration flight in a two-seater Fury which Bill Humble had delivered a year or two before. My next trip was by road to Swat, to meet the Prince who had presented the Fury I had flown out to the RPAF. As we drove through the passes and foothills and well into Kipling country we saw the crests of many famous British regiments cut into the hillsides. Tribesmen armed with Bataan knives, rifles and ammunition gave an atmosphere of tribal war. We drove round hairpin bends in rugged precipitous country swept by gusty winds and reached the village of Swat to be received by the Prince in a modern palace. He was charming, and presented me with a jade-handled dagger before leaving.

Before returning to Peshawar I visited Chaklala and spent a rather uneasy night after learning that my hut was surrounded by long grass favoured by cobras. I do not like snakes. Back at Peshawar I had a flight up to Gilgit, near Kashmir. As our Bristol Freighter flew up ravines, hillsides towered high above and narrowed in places to about a mile wide.

A few days later I was back at Bray again, celebrating the new records at a dinner at the "Hind's Head" with Gwen, having returned to London Airport in twenty-five hours by the normal BOAC service. Pakistan seemed almost a dream.

While I had been away Wimpy Wade had also established a record, from London to Paris in the P1052 on May 13th. Haze delayed take-off but Frank Murphy, checking the weather in a Sea Fury, found that visibility was improving outside the London Airport area. Wimpy flew to Villa Coublay, a flight of 221 miles, in 21 minutes 27.6 seconds, an average speed of 618 miles an hour, and clipped 6 minutes 9.7 seconds off the previous record by Bill Waterton in a Meteor 7 the previous December. Bad weather prevented Wimpy from attempting a record on the return flight; nevertheless he managed to get back in 23 minutes 30 seconds.

I had enjoyed the flight to Karachi, and when Furies were ordered by the Royal Egyptian Air Force we felt that here was another opportunity of showing what Hawker aircraft could do. I began flight planning again, and decided to leave from Blackbushe, travelling to Almaza either via Bari or Malta. The Bari route was 130 miles shorter, but I preferred Malta. The distance from Blackbushe is 1,310 miles and it was estimated that the Fury could cover it in 3 hours 40 minutes and still have a reserve of 43 gallons of fuel. The time taken was 3 hours 36 minutes and there were 40 gallons to spare. From Malta to Almaza is 1,055 miles and the estimate here was 2 hours 43 minutes. The actual time returned was 2 hours 44 minutes.

Prior to the flight, much time was spent studying the weather and wind speeds and the direction of winds in the upper air. Maps were marked showing the track to be followed and the times that the Fury should be over certain points. Finally everything was settled. I was to take off on February 16th, 1950.

My pyjamas, shirts, shoes, trousers, toothbrush and razor were stuffed into the gun bays of the Fury and any small angular corners; then I flew over to Blackbushe from Langley. There was a mass of paper work to get through that evening—customs clearance, immigration, flight plans, refuelling. The meteorological forecast also had to be studied.

I spent the night in Camberley and it was still dark when I reached the airfield the following morning. The ground crew had already run up the engine. The fuel tanks were brimming over. Bert Hayward loaned me his lucky farthing again. Gwen, Wimpy and the directors were there to say good-bye.

Take-off was at 7.41 a.m. I made a right-hand turn and was over the starting line below 300 feet a minute later. Climbing through cloud between 2,000 and 5,000 feet, I went up to my cruising height of 21,000 feet and, after flying above cloud and in sunshine for an hour and twenty minutes, pin-pointed Lyons under clear skies. Skirting Grenoble I had a magnificent view of the Alps, the sun glinting on their snowy slopes, and visibility was now so clear that I could see the south coast of France.

Cannes slipped by eight minutes ahead of schedule; Corsica came up and disappeared; Sardinia faded away and forty minutes later Sicily was ringed with thunderstorms—correctly forecast. With cloud, bumps and a change in the direction of the wind, the Fury's speed was reduced. When, estimating that I was fifteen minutes away from Malta, I began to let down, the windcreen started to mist and to ice-up; but this had been anticipated and I rubbed the front screen with a rag soaked in glycol and was able to peer out to where the island should be. Soon, through the rain, Luqa airfield, spouting yellow Very lights showing which runway to use, lay below.

Once again the RAF and the Shell Company worked quickly and smoothly. Petrol bowsers swarmed round the Fury and three hundred and forty gallons were pumped in six minutes. It was good to sight Fred Sutton in the crowd—he had been sent out by Hawker's to supervise the servicing and did an excellent job. It seemed to me that, before I had hardly stretched myself, I was thrust bodily back into the cockpit, a full weather briefing with wind speeds and directions pushed into my hands, and I was off again. After being on the ground for sixteen minutes the runway was tearing past, and Malta in retrospect was a blur of rain, faces, bowsers and hot coffee—which I had not time to drink.

Sorting things out in the cockpit needed a little time, but it was soon plain that the weather forecast was accurate. It said that there would be much cloud from Luqa to El Adem and rain with moderate icing, some turbulence and a risk of severe icing and turbulence. The clouds went up to 26,000 feet, and it was a bumpy ride skimming along just above their peaks. This unexpected climbing upset the estimated time of arrival over the African coast by a minute and a half but conditions were perfect above Gazala, and from now on it was necessary only to check course, position and time and to estimate ground speed. Gazala and then Tobruk, Gambut and Sollum slipped by and my thoughts went back to the days with 112 and 92 Squadrons. The desert was unchanged, but now there were no 109's about.

The Fury hummed along. Everything was working out according to our estimates. Bardia, Sidi Barrani, Mersa Matruh came up at the right times, and in the right places, the coastline gradually faded away to the north, and I turned south of El Alamein and headed out over the sandy wastes of Wadi Natruñ. Thin layers of cloud at 15,000 feet did not interfere with a position-check at the Alexandria–Cairo road; I put down the nose about ten minutes away from Almaza and then, descending through cloud, I saw Cairo again, with all its sand and coloured houses, for the first time in six years, and Heliopolis and Almaza straight ahead. The Fury passed the finishing line 6 hours 32 minutes 10 seconds after leaving Blackbushe; its average speed had been 360 miles an hour, including the refuelling stop at Luqa. It was another record: it stood until April 24th, 1950 when John Cunningham flew the Comet to Cairo in 5 hours 6 minutes 58.3 seconds.

There was a reception by high ranking officers of the Royal Egyptian Air Force and some leading civil aviation people, and representatives of the Royal Aero Club of Egypt checked the official seals on the engine and the aircraft. I was glad to see that the engine seal had not worked loose. I did not want to be suspected of changing an engine *en route!* I spent two weeks with the Royal Egyptian Air Force, converting some of their pilots to the Fury before returning to Bray.

These two flights had been interesting diversions from experimental and production test flying. Equally pleasant changes were taking part in races. Wimpy, Frank Murphy, Doc Morrell and I were entered for the first of the post-war national races, held at Elmdon, near Birmingham, in August 1949. I flew the P1040 and Frank a Sea Fury trainer for the Kemsley Challenge Trophy on the Saturday, and on August Bank Holiday, Wimpy flew the P1040 for the Society of British Aircraft Constructors' Trophy. Doc Morrell took part in the Air League Challenge Trophy Race in the Sea Fury.

The races took place over a twenty mile rectangular course. The first leg was a run of 5 miles to Knowle, the second of 6.4 miles to Corley, the third of 4.3 miles to Coleshill, and the final run back from Coleshill to Elmdon was also 4.3 miles. Sodium flares were laid at the turns and they were a great help; we had to keep an eye on electric grid lines, some of them rising to 100 feet, at various points. I went round the course several times in Furies before taking up the P1040, for local knowledge is important in a race. The jet went well during the practice laps and, with the right amount of G at the turns, lost comparatively little speed. In the Kemsley Trophy race, Frank Murphy and I had ranged against us John Cunningham, flying a Vampire for de Havillands; Group Captain A H Wheeler in a Spitfire 5 and Guy Morgan in a Spitfire trainer, entered by Supermarines; P G Lawrence in a Firebrand, flying for Blackburns. R W Jamieson flew a Hornet, also for de Havillands. The event was open to any aircraft with a maximum speed at sea-level exceeding 300 miles per hour. All were given a handicap, and I was scratch machine.

The piston-engined aircraft went off first and John Cunningham and I sat in the cockpits of our aircraft and watched the field come round at the end of the first of four circuits. Then John went off and I followed him. I left the throttle of the P1040 wide open, but I had to pass all the aircraft except the Vampire twice and it was not until the last lap that I could be sure of my prospects. The final leg from Coleshill to Elmdon was most exciting. I could now pick out Frank and John ahead of me and, with all the other aircraft apparently massed together, the P1040 tore through them. As we passed over the finishing line it seemed that there was not much to choose between us.

It was not until I landed that I learned that the P1040 had arrived one second in front of John Cunningham's Vampire, and that John had finished three seconds ahead of Frank Murphy's Sea Fury trainer. It was a handicap event and the average speed of the P1040 was given officially as 508 miles per hour with a time of 16 minutes 24 seconds. John Cunningham averaged 470 miles per hour in 16 minutes 25 seconds, and Frank Murphy 340 miles per hour in 16 minutes 28 seconds. Frank had flown a very good race, and during his second lap he pulled his aircraft so smartly round the Coleshill turn that he blacked out temporarily and lost a second or two.

"I reckon you chaps cost me £50 a second in prize money," he told John and me later. Until the last few moments of the race he had been leading.

The P1040 went round one lap at an average of 562.569 miles per hour and at times the speed was over 600 miles per hour.

On August Bank Holiday, when there was a crowd estimated at about 100,000 we saw Wimpy, John Cunningham and John Derry give excellent performances in the SBAC race. John Derry was at scratch in the de Havilland 108 and went off 1 minute 3 seconds after John Cunningham in his Vampire. Wimpy, with 16 seconds start on John Derry, got everything out of the P1040 to win with an average speed of 510 miles per hour. We were interested to find that his fastest lap was exactly the same as mine, to one-thousandths of a mile per hour:

562.569 miles per hour. Cunningham's average was 470 miles per hour and Derry's 488 miles per hour. Wimpy and I shared the Geoffrey de Havilland Memorial Trophy for the fastest lap; and we were well pleased with the Elmdon results, for Hawker's had also collected two firsts and a third.

CHAPTER 12

# Test Pilot

HAWKER'S development work was at a most interesting stage when I joined the firm in August 1948. They had produced their first jet fighter, the P1040, to the specifications of the Air Ministry, designed by their brilliant team headed by Sir Sydney Camm, CBE, whose Hurricane took such an important part in winning the Battle of Britain. Sydney Camm is a tremendous character with a vast wealth of aeronautical experience.

In certain respects the P1040 was an unorthodox aircraft for, although fitted with a single Rolls-Royce Nene engine with twin intakes at the wing roots, it had a split jet pipe with two exhausts at the wing root trailing edge on either side of the fuselage; it also had straight wings, a straight tail and a normal fin. It was a beautiful aircraft to fly with spring tab ailerons, and it attracted the attention of the Admiralty. The Royal Navy took it over, converted it for deck-landings with the addition of a hook, and gave it folding wings and other nautical refinements. This version of the P1040 became known as the N7/46, and was later produced as the Seahawk. It is now in service with the Fleet Air Arm.

After the P1040 came the P1052, with a number of important changes in design. Two of these aircraft were built for research purposes, with thirty-five degree swept-back wings—the first used by Hawker's—and much the same engine lay-out as the P1040. After some development work, one of the P1052's was converted into the P1081. This was fully swept-back on all surfaces, and the engine layout was changed: instead of the split or bifurcated jet pipe, the engine had a straight-through jet pipe, exhausting in a single pipe under the tail.

Both the P1052 and the P1081 were used for research only, and no production was begun, although it would have been a comparatively

142

simple matter to convert them to fighters. They were two of the first aircraft with swept-back wings in the country; and we began to use them for research into high Mach number flight. Until then the highest Mach number reached in England had been 0.8-odd with speeds around 600 miles per hour. With the P1052 we were able to reach more than Mach go at height, and airspeeds of well over 600 miles per hour at sea-level, after we had ironed out various things which could cause buffeting. It was about this time that John Derry went through the sonic barrier for the first time in a De Havilland 108, a swept-back tail-less aircraft with a Goblin engine.

While work was proceeding with the P1052 and the P1081 we also tried out the Snarler rocket on the P1040 which, with this addition, became the P1072. The Snarler was an Armstrong-Siddeley rocket installation fitted to the tail of the aircraft, the idea being to get the rocket airborne for experimental engine development. We assessed the results of its performance and power in a series of climbs.

Wimpy Wade and I made three flights each with the Snarler, and found that it gave the P1072 terrific climb performance, particularly at height. We took off normally on the jet engine, and then lit the rocket at a fairly low altitude, putting the aircraft into a climb. With the Nene jet engine working at full power, together with the thrust of the rocket, the aircraft went up extremely rapidly.

There were two points we had to watch: that we did not exceed the Mach number of which the aircraft was capable; and that we did not climb beyond 40,000 feet—the aircraft had no pressurized cabin and it is unsafe to fly above that height unless the cabin is pressurized or the pilot wears a pressure suit.

During my last flight with the rocket, I was re-lighting it between 3,000 and 10,000 feet when the thing exploded and set fire to the tail of the aircraft. I could see in my cockpit mirror just what was going on, so I shut down the rocket and landed. The burning tail of the aircraft evidently looked worse from the ground than it seemed while I was in the air.

The use of rocket propelled fighters for interceptor work has, I think, interesting possibilities. The big advantage of a rocket is that it drives an aircraft along with exactly the same power at 5,000 feet as it does at 50,000 feet or more. On the other hand a jet engine has approximately only one-fifth of its sea-level power at 50,000 feet. The basic difference is that a rocket carries its own power while a jet engine relies on the outside air to give it power; and at heights of 55,000 feet and above, the air is so thin that a jet cannot suck in sufficient air to maintain its efficiency.

With rocket power and an aircraft of the right design it is possible to reach tremendous speeds at heights above 40,000 feet where air density is low and resistance to the flight or passage through the air of an aircraft is very small. In fact speeds of about 1,000 to 1,600 miles per hour have already been recorded.

With a rocket-propelled fighter it would be possible to reach a height of 50,000 feet in about three-and-a-half minutes, including take-off time, and this would be a most useful performance for defence against modern bombers approaching at around 600 miles per hour. There would be various problems to overcome; for instance, once the rocket's power had been used up, the aircraft could only be glided around which would cause complications such as becoming too easy a prey for escorting fighters. A small jet engine is desirable for descent and landing, particularly in bad weather.

With our development work on the P1052 and P1081 we reached high Mach numbers, and to compile information we began to use a wire-recorder installed in the aircraft. One day, while Wimpy and I were chatting with John Derry and John Cunningham, we mentioned the value of the wire-recorder.

"This sounds most interesting. Could we come over to Langley and hear a play-back," John Derry asked us.

"By all means."

Wimpy and I decided that we might make a special recording for our two friends.

We set up the recorder in Wimpy's office; and in the next room we started up a vacuum cleaner. Wimpy talked into the recorder and when we played it back, the noise of the cleaner in the next room sounded very much like the noise of a jet engine from the cockpit, and, with his comments, was a good imitation of the real thing. So Wimpy went to work and made a fairly good length recording of an imaginary flight.

We rang up the two Johns.

"Come over any time you like," Wimpy told them.

The four of us got together in Wimpy's office; and we began to play back.

Derry and Cunningham seemed most impressed, particularly when Wimpy's voice was heard saying:

"Diving now . . . Mach point eight . . . eight five . . . nine . . . nine five . . . nine seven . . . nine eight . . . nine nine . . ."

In fact we had not pushed the P1052 anywhere near that Mach number, and both John Derry and John Cunningham began to look not only interested but astonished, though trying to appear unconcerned.

It may have been our amusement at their expressions or else they caught Wimpy exchanging glances with me; but it wasn't long before they twigged that they were somewhere down the end of the garden path. Anyway, we provided them with some beer and explained that we had exaggerated a little but that we did really find the recorder useful.

Shortly after this, early in 1951, Wimpy left for the United States under a "scheme" for the exchange of civilian test pilots. He had been sent there by Hawker's to gain experience on Amercian jet aircraft. While he was away I had been flying the P1081 on developmental work.

"I think I'll go over to Farnborough and see how you have been getting on with the 1081," Wimpy said to me shortly after his return to Langley.

We never knew what happened. The aircraft crashed at Lewes, in Sussex, and was a complete write off. Wimpy baled out, using his ejector seat from which he did not release himself. I had lost another close friend, of 92 Squadron and my first days at Biggin, and it was a sad moment when I went with John Lidbury, secretary to Hawker's, to break the news to Josephine. Wimpy was a first-class pilot, a great personality, and his work contributed to the knowledge of the company in producing the Hunter.

During the middle of April 1951 I was appointed to succeed Wimpy as chief test pilot, but any pride or pleasure I took in the appointment— and I regarded it as a great honour—was sadly marred by his death which we all felt very much. It was not the only loss for Josephine; one of her three children, Michael, died quite suddenly a short time later. It was an unhappy period.

## CHAPTER 13

# Chief Test Pilot

MY appointment as chief test pilot came when 615 was about to begin three months' continuous training, due to the Korean war, and I found it quite impossible to be responsible for all the flying at Hawker's and to continue as commanding officer of the squadron. Though I was distressed, there was no other course than resignation from 615. In due time I handed over to Squadron Leader Freddie Sowrey, DFC, a regular RAF officer. I informed Sir Winston Churchill, as honorary air commodore, of my decision and the reasons for it, and I was touched when he took the trouble to answer my letter while he was on holiday in Annecy, in France, and invited me to keep in touch with him. I was able to be at Biggin when he made an official visit during 615's continuous training; and I have been transferred to the Royal Auxiliary Air Force Reserve of Officers until September 16th, 1960. I keep contact with the squadron and Biggin; in 1952 I went to see 615 in their summer camp at Celle, flying over Germany in our Hurricane "The Last of the Many". During a squadron function last autumn Sir Winston presented Gwen and me to Queen Elizabeth the Queen Mother, a great honour.

There have been other changes. After our lease of the house at Bray expired, we moved to the sixteenth century "Thatched Cottage", Upper Bourne End, not far from Maidenhead, high above the Thames. Late in 1951 Hawker's took over the former RAF airfield at Dunsfold, near Godalming, for the Langley airfield is rather too near London Airport both for our comfort and for that of the civil airlines. Early in January, 1952, we moved into an old farmhouse, part of it going back to the sixteenth century, just off the Dunsfold perimeter track. It had been used as an RAF headquarters during the war but had become badly dilapidated; yet Gwen, with her excellent artistic taste, has transformed it into the most comfortable of homes, and it is one of the pleasures of life during winter to be able to toast our toes in front of a large inglenook fireplace, burning two-foot logs. A mile further along the perimeter track Frank and Gloria Murphy live with their two children. Our houses are pleasantly close to the control tower, though our wives are rather cut off from the outside world, particularly as all visitors have to pass guards on the gates.

From time to time there have been changes on the test pilot's staff. Doc Morrell left in 1951 and began flying at Hamble. We were joined as my No. 2 by Bill Bedford, who served on Hurricanes in Burma during the war, and was later an instructor at the Empire Test Pilots' School, being awarded the AFC. Bill shares the responsibilities of experimental flying with me, and he spends many of his weekends gliding at Farnborough with pilots of the Royal Aircraft Establishment. He holds several height and distance gliding records, and, being a qualified instructor, passes on his valuable experience to pupils in a two-seater glider.

Frank Bullen also joined us as a production test pilot. He flew Spitfires and Mustangs with No. 11 Group of Fighter Command during the war and, for a period, was personal assistant to Air Marshal Sir James Robb at 11 Group Headquarters at Stanmore. He came to us during 1949 after two-and-a-half years with Blackburn's as a test pilot. A newcomer to our test team is Donald Lucey ex-Fleet Air Arm.

With Frank Murphy, we are a fairly small flying team at Dunsfold. We work together in the control tower with the flying control staff, headed by Bertie Coopman, a former squadron leader, and Bill Willis, his assistant; and also with the technical staff of the flight test section headed by Fred Sutton.

We can test fly in most weather conditions for, with de Havillands and Supermarines, we operate a private fixer service. We also have an automatic homing device and a form of controlling descents when the weather is poor or indifferent. We sometimes fly at night and at this time the air is calm and stable and would be suitable for tests such as performance measurement.

The flight test programmes are arranged by the flight test section which also looks after aircraft instrumentation and the automatic recording instruments as well as analysing or reducing our test results. Fred Sutton invariably tucks us into the aircraft with a few final words of instruction and receives our reports as soon as we land.

There is a routine about test flying, and it goes something along these lines:

The day at Dunsfold begins with the provision of a weather forecast by Bertie Coopman, and with this we also receive a list of aircraft available for flying both at Dunsfold and Langley, where Sea Furies are flight-tested. If the weather is suitable for flying, we have a conference in my office with the pilots and Fred Sutton to arrange the flying programme.

Fred Sutton may report that four Furies will be ready at Langley at 11 o'clock and that two production Seahawks will be available at Dunsfold. As chief production test pilot Frank Murphy arranges for a Rapide to be provided to take him and Frank Bullen to Langley to clear the Furies; or he may decide to send Bullen to Langley and to deal with the Seahawks himself at Dunsfold.

If Fred Sutton says:

"One Hunter, 202, will be ready during the late morning for levels at 35 and 40,000 feet. Here is the flight programme. A full throttle climb to 50,000 feet is required." I decide to do this trip, while realising that "late morning" usually seems to mean the middle of lunchtime! I ask that the oxygen system in the Hunter, which is the Sapphire-engined Mark II version, be set to pressure breathing, for the flight will take me up to 50,000 feet or more and I shall want to use the pressure waistcoat. Fred gives me the appropriate climbing speeds and a briefing form which provides details of the aircraft's weight, centre of gravity and fuel load, together with any changes made to the aircraft since it was last flown; it also provides a note on engine or airframe limitations if they should not be normal, and a programme of the tests I am to do and what power is to be used. He will also expect a record of the air temperature during the Hunter's descent so that the performance figures noted can be reduced accurately to standard conditions.

Fred Sutton may also say:

"195 will also be ready by mid-morning and they want the stability tests at 5,000 and 35,000 feet completed as soon as possible." By "195" he means an Avon-engined Hunter Mark I, and by "they" he indicates our design department at Kingston. Bill Bedford has been doing these stability tests and, since it is preferable for one pilot to complete a full set using the same technique throughout, this will be his job. We find that we get more consistent results in stability tests by the same pilot completing a series, for they involve stick force per G and also acceleration in and out of trim dives, which can be influenced in their final results by the technique of the pilot.

We agree that the flying at 5,000 feet should be done first while the weather is clear, for it may clamp down a bit this particular afternoon.

With the conference ended and when everybody has gone off to their own offices, I settle down to deal with the morning's paper work which is steadily increasing with the Hunters coming along into production. It may also include replying to small boys who always seem to want vast numbers of photographs of Hawker aircraft, ancient and modern.

Then I get down to planning my coming flight in "202". I write the climb speed figures and other relevant points on my test pad, checking its stop-watch and seeing that it is working properly—it would be a bit late to discover that it was not going once I had started a full throttle climb in the Hunter. It climbs so fast that you don't have time to correct mistakes once you have begun to go up. The pressure waistcoat also has to be checked, and tested if necessary; the oxygen mask to be used with the waistcoat must be attached to my American protective flying helmet. Then there are overalls and gloves to be collected, maps folded, pencils sharpened, and perhaps a second look at the test pad to make sure that it has a full roll of paper, for it would be infuriating to find that you have used up all the notepaper while still having many points to jot down. I also check up on the weather and the wind to decide the geographical direction in which to make the climb and carry out the level speed runs which take up a lot of country.

Some days tick by smoothly without hitches; others not so smoothly, for experimental aircraft require careful inspection and no definite time can always be given for take-off if unexpected faults are discovered. Waiting around for aircraft seems to be common to all forms of aviation. Somehow or other it often seems that experimental flying is done at the end of the day or during week-ends; but an aircraft must be flown when it is ready. And if your programme is to move forward steadily you have to be prepared to fly at any time.

An efficient secretary is of infinite value in a test pilot's life, and I was fortunate in having Mrs Maureen Sterling to help me. She deals with anything that is fiddling or worrying or distracting during the day; and, when the wire recorder has been used during experimental flights, she plays it back and types out my comments and is tactfully deaf to any stray adjectives that may have crept in.

I find that it is a great advantage to live on the aerodrome, for at any time during the week-end when we are flying I can look out of my window and see if an aircraft is ready, and wander across to the hangars. As a change from test-flying and to give us a taste of cloth cap-and-goggle flying we use our private Hawker museum of interesting types, which, to my mind, are magnificent aircraft. There is the Hawker Cygnet, vintage 192, the first aircraft which Sir Sydney Camm had a hand in designing. It has a little 36 hp Bristol Cherub engine, a top speed of 75 miles per hour, drooping ailerons which can be wound down as flaps. This type of full span, narrow chord aileron may be seen on very fast aircraft again shortly. This Cygnet, flown by George Bulman, won the light aeroplane contest at Lympne in the 'twenties. Then there is the Hawker Hart light bomber, born during the early 'thirties, which causes a certain nostalgia among many older service pilots whenever we land it at their stations. There is also the Tomtit. Both the Hart and the Tomtit have variable incidence tailplanes which may be seen on the Hunter. We also have a Hurricane "The Last of the Many" and one of only two surviving to this day in this country, two Rapides, one Avro 19, a Miles Whitney Straight and, at Langley, a Sabre-engined Fury which I hope we shall get into the air again one day.

We fly these various types on demonstrations and at displays during the summer. The Hurricane we use for liaison visits to the RAF and the RN Squadrons; the Avro, which has a Decca navigator and a flight log, for flying our directors at any time of the night or day and in all weathers; and the Whitney Straight has taken Gwen and me abroad three times for holidays, to Africa and Spain and France.

Another interest has been experience of deck landings on aircraft carriers. In January 1949, I went to Milltown with Geoffrey Pike, of de Havillands, on a course. We spent a week practising "addles"—aerodrome dummy deck landings—in Firefly I's and were then taken aboard a destroyer in the Moray Firth, where we stayed the night and I slept on the chart table, before going on board HMS *Implacable*. Geoffrey and I made four landings in a Firefly under the eye of Commander J C Cockburn, DSO, and the commanding officer of the *Implacable's* Hornet Squadron, Lieutenant Commander R. Law, DSC, RN.

I met Dickie Law again in July, 1952 at Boscombe Down when I brushed up my dummy landings in a Meteor before going aboard the *Illustrious* off Selsey Bill. The Navy wasted no time. I was picked up at Dunsfold by Lieutenant "Slim" Sear in a Firefly at 1.30 pm. He flew me to the carrier in half an hour. I was back at Dunsfold again by 4 pm having made five landings on the *Illustrious* in a Meteor without any extraordinary incidents. Landing on a carrier as a passenger in a Firefly is interesting. The passenger can see only to either side of the cockpit; he watches the sea coming closer, he notices the wash of the ship, and finally there is a bump and a squeak of rubber tyres on the deck. These landings have a technique of their own which is interesting to learn. I always enjoy my visits to the Royal Navy during Seahawk trials on aircraft carriers. Flying and the sea make, to my mind, a grand combination.

Towards the end of 1949 the mock-up stage of the Hunter was reached. The mock-up is the building of the prototype in wood—mostly three-ply—and it is from this stage onwards that the chief test pilot is called in fairly regularly; until now he has probably been consulted about things like cockpit lay-out and the position of controls and instruments.

Once the mock-up stage is reached, he is able to get into the cockpit and give his opinions on matters such as the view from the pilot's seat, the comfort of the cabin, ease of getting in or out, and the lay-out of controls, instruments, flap and under-carriage selectors, oxygen equipment, emergency systems and so forth. The mock-up is being changed constantly, not only because of different Air Ministry requirements, but also because of any ideas the design team may have and, of course in our case, from the experience we have gained with the earlier aircraft. We still have the mock-up of the Hunter, and still change it. While Wimpy was alive he took part in the discussions with the designers as chief test pilot. When I succeeded him after his death, the Hunter was in the cockpit lay-out stage; and I remember that we made various changes in the position of certain instruments and other minor alterations such as the repositioning of fuel cocks to make them more accessible. A cockpit has to be easily adaptable for short and tall pilots and adjustment to seats and pedals is provided to cope with the various lengths.

The construction of the Hunter proceeded throughout 1950, and by spring of 1951, it began to take a very definite shape. As the weeks passed and the final jobs were started, such as the wing and fuselage skinning, wiring, control system functioning, engine installation and fuel system tests, you could notice that everybody was beginning to get a little more tensed up. To prepare for flying the Hunter, I gave myself some initial training. I flew a Canberra with Avon engines to verse myself in engine handling, stopping and relighting in the air, and so on. I flew the American F 86A or Sabre, and found it a most pleasant aircraft. I went over to Farnborough and was fixed up with the Martin Baker ejector seat rig, just in case anything should go wrong with the Hunter. From the Institute of Aviation Medicine I obtained an American flying helmet. It is of the protective, or crash, type and although heavy, weighing four to four and a half pounds, I find it comfortable. It provides protection during flight at high speed in turbulent air, when there is a danger of striking your head on the canopy; and it would certainly be useful in a crash or in the event of canopy failure. I am very much in favour of these helmets. The Institute also fitted me with a pressure waistcoat and mask; and I went through the pressure chamber at simulated heights up to 50,000 feet.

At last the day came when the Hunter was moved from Kingston to Boscombe Down, where many prototypes in England make their first flight, for the airfield has one of the longest runways in the country—3,000 yards—and is most useful for taxi trials and initial flights.

It was now June and, for about three weeks, Bill Turner and his team worked on the aircraft, and the engineers spent long hours on the Rolls-Royce Avon engine, running it for prolonged periods and seeing that the structure of the airframe round the jet pipe and engine was getting sufficient cooling.

Finally the Hunter was ready for taxi trials. It looked a beautiful aircraft as I walked over to it, standing just outside a hangar. It was painted a pale, duck-egg green, with RAF roundels on the wings and fuselage; its wings were swept and there was a graceful sweep up to the tail, the engine exhausted in a straight jet pipe under the rudder.

I was in my full flying kit. It was unnecessary, speaking strictly, to wear all this gear; but it is advisable to do so at this stage to make yourself at home in the cockpit and also to make certain finally that you can reach all the controls easily despite all your bulky equipment.

I climbed up the metal ladder, settled myself in, started the engine and began the first taxiing at slow speeds along the runway. You always

30.,

The red Hawker Hunter WB 188, in which we set the world speed record for a closed circuit, in September, 1953.

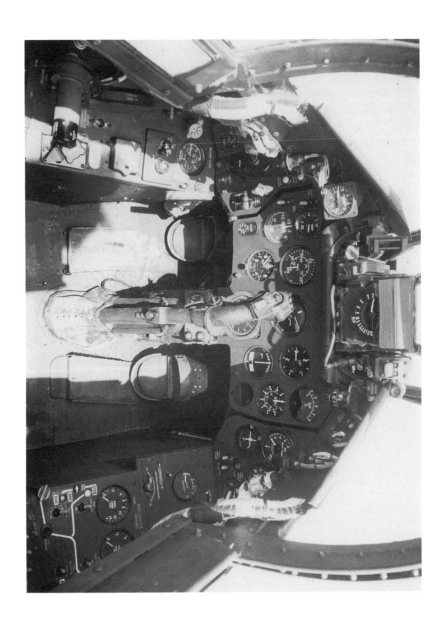

31.,

"The office"—cockpit of the Hunter fighter.

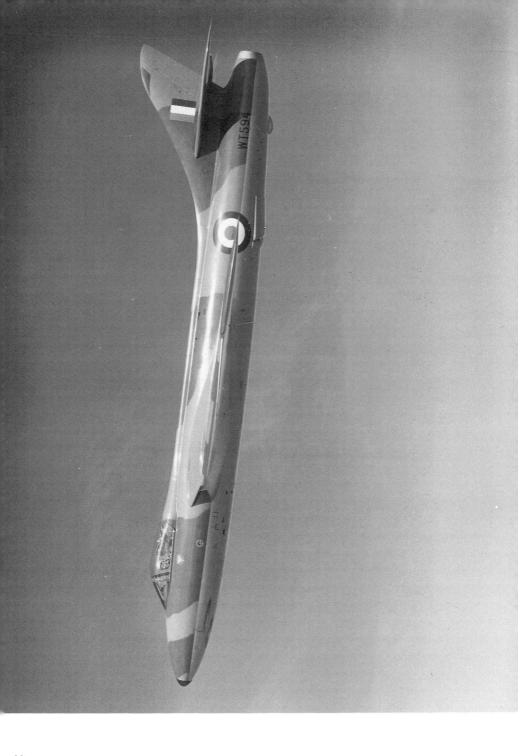

32.

Hawker Hunter in RAF "warpaint" — ready for squadron service.

33.,

WB 195 heading down.

34.

The beautiful lines of the Hunter in flight.

35.,

Prototype Hawker P1052.

work to a programme from the moment you step into a prototype for the first time. After a series of slow taxiing testing the Hunter's manoeuvrability on the ground, I opened the throttle a little more and began moving the aircraft faster along the runway checking for shimmy or snatching on the brakes.

From the first I felt at home in the Hunter. Gradually I worked up to fast runs, noting over the wire-recorder the speed at which the nose wheel came off the ground and the speed at which the elevators and the rudder became effective.

Then the time came to try a short hop—to get the "unstick" speed and correct trimmer setting and the feel of the controls. To work up sufficient speed for even a short hop you need quite a distance and despite the Boscombe Down 3,000 yard runway, I had covered a lot of ground by the time I eased back the control column. The Hunter hopped satisfactorily and I was happy about the feel of the controls. I touched down, throttled back; but the end of the runway was approaching very quickly. With the highish idling thrust of the Avon engine, far more powerful than anything I had handled until now, the Hunter continued to move more quickly than I wished. I could see the end of the runway coming up and its grass overshoot—and, beyond the grass, hedges and ditches.

I braked as hard as I could and by the time the end of the runway was reached the Hunter was moving sufficiently slowly for me to slew it round and run down the perimeter track. I noticed a fire engine tearing round towards me—its crew being able to see what I could not: the brakes were smouldering with clouds of bluish smoke. They had burned right out, but it was a comparatively simple matter to fit a new set of wheels and brakes—certainly far more simple than having to iron out the bruises we should have collected if the Hunter had gone past the grass overshoot of the runway. We made a note that the time seems to be past when you can do hops with high powered prototypes unless you have a tremendously long runway.

After a few more successful taxi trials, the Hunter was ready for the first flight. But not quite. Day after day for nearly a week, I went over to Boscombe from Langley expecting to take off; but the experimental flight team was taking no chances and was making the most thorough and careful inspection. They were determined to get it on the top-line and always, it seemed, some detail required fixing. Some three years' hard work had gone into the Hunter, it represented an enormous amount of thinking, skill and capital. Any hitch now would put back its programme by perhaps months.

Finally, one day in July, we got the green light. We took off from Langley in a Rapide and in it were Mr Neville Spriggs, OBE, the general manager of Hawker's, Mr Roy Chaplin, assistant chief designer, Mr Donald Stranks, the chief experimental engineer, and Mr Frank Cross, of the experimental drawing office. Mr Camm said that he would drive over to Boscombe in his car, though there seemed some doubt as to whether he would be able to get away.

When we landed we learned that there was still some work to be done on the Hunter. A party of us drove into Amesbury for tea, but I remember I had no particular appetite. Quite frankly, I was a little tense. The Hunter had been in the thoughts of all of us for so long and I had had so much to do with it, that I was tremendously keen to fly it. I had never taken up a prototype on its maiden flight. . . .

The day drags on . . . it won't be ready until evening. There seem to be hundreds of people about, all wanting to chat about this and that. I wish there weren't so many . . . I'd much prefer to fly it off without anybody standing around . . . I wish I didn't have to chatter so much . . . I suppose that fuel system will be all right . . . and the controls. Not much need to worry about engine failure.

"It'll be ready at seven o'clock."

Hell, not before then . . . seems hours. Still the time is passing.

"Ready now, Mr Duke."

This is it. Out we go. Got everything . . . flight programme . . . knee pad and stopwatch . . . helmet and gloves? Yes. All OK.

Leave the office . . . seems a nice warm evening . . . bit of cloud around 15,000 feet . . . there it is, pale green, a beauty.

Nobody is talking . . . everything seems deathly quiet . . . try to look unconcerned but I can't help feeling selfconscious . . . wish they wouldn't stare at me. Up the ladder and settle myself in, with the ground crew making the odd joke while fixing my harness . . . plug in the oxygen and r/t . . . wire-recorder "on". Now then, let's see.

You forget everything and everybody while you go through the cockpit drill. . . . Check the hydraulic system by lowering the flaps, check the trimmers for full and correct movement . . . work the controls and engage the power system . . . turn on the oxygen and test it . . . straps tight and seat adjusted. Everything seems all right.

Start up the Avon . . . watch the temperatures and pressure . . . everything is working . . . shut the hood . . . adjust the oxygen mask and helmet strap. Right. Wave the chocks away. Start taxiing . . . down the perimeter track with everything working nicely . . . pull up by the end of the runway. I can see the hangars about a quarter of a mile away with a knot of people; a number of cars moving off to gather either side of the runway, about half-way down. It is a nice, clear evening . . . and the runway looks comfortably long; in any case I can't see the end because it's the other side of the slope. Time to call up control.

" 'Hawker Baker' calling Boscombe Tower. Am I clear to taxi on?" Hawker Baker is my call sign.

"Baker clear to line-up and take-off."

Move on to the end of the runway . . . let's have another complete and thorough check up . . . everything seems right.

Now!

Open up the throttle, holding the brakes on . . . revs and jet pipe temperature sliding up as they should . . . quite a whine from the engine . . . more throttle . . . we're moving even on the brakes. One more quick check up. All OK. Off we go.

Brakes off and full throttle . . . tremendous acceleration. Keep her straight . . . good. Now start chattering on the wire-recorder . . . mention the speed at which the rudder and elevators begin to become effective . . . speed at which the nose-wheel lifts . . . engine revs per minute and jet pipe temperature . . . speed of the "unstick". We're up . . . every sense alert for the slightest fault . . . part of the aircraft in feel, sound, sight and smell.

It is a nice, smooth, easy take-off, with speed increasing remarkably quickly. Don't raise the under-carriage just yet in case there may be some change in trim . . . 500 feet . . . up with the wheels. Ease back on the throttle, we're not out for speed on this trip . . . 250 knots, that'll do . . . up, up in a steady climb, 10,000 feet . . . 15,000 feet . . . let's dodge those clouds . . . 20,000 feet. That'll do. That must be Bournemouth below . . . let's sheer over towards Southampton and then back to the Boscombe area in case a hasty landing is necessary.

It handles beautifully and you get a sudden feeling of exhilaration. You've got it up all right with no hitches and the initial tension is over. Now go through the flight programme. Good . . . good . . . h'm.. . . Let's see how it'll go on a simulated landing approach, it's safe enough at this

height anyway, even if there are hitches. Wheels down . . . flaps down
. . . throttle back . . . trim back a bit. Seems OK.

Look at the time! Been up for nearly an hour . . . time to return to
base. Come down gradually . . . yes, that's Boscombe.

"Hawker Baker calling Boscombe tower. Joining circuit."

"Baker, you are clear to join. Runway two-four."

Wide, gentle circuit and a long, smooth approach. Keep the speed up
a bit, we don't want it to stall and there's plenty of runway. Down we
come . . . check, easing back gently on the stick as the speed falls off. . . .
A light rumble as the wheels make contact . . . that's it. Taxiing now
. . . look at those cars shooting over to the hangars. Open the hood. Flaps
up. Fresh air is grand. Round we go . . . up to the hangars . . . what a
crowd . . . pull her up and shut down.

How quiet everything seems. Nobody's saying a word . . . just
staring. . . . Off helmet and test pad. Out we get, down the ladder . . . still
nobody speaks, it seems even quieter than when I got in . . . must say
something.

"Jolly good!"

And then babel breaks out. Everybody starts talking, asking
questions and you chat and chat. Everybody seems to be smiling, and I
must say I feel pretty pleased myself, but a bit hot.

I certainly enjoyed that first flight in the Hunter, but I was sorry about
one thing. As we took off in the Rapide to return to Langley we heard
that Sydney Camm was just arriving. If I'd known he was coming for
sure I would have delayed my take-off.

I flew the Hunter about six times at Boscombe, working to flight
programmes and increasing gradually the speed and height and trying
it out in stalls. Then I flew it over to Dunsfold to begin the
development programme. There were, of course, all sorts of things to
be ironed out before we could start working up towards high Mach
numbers, but then there always are a few teething troubles with most
new types of aircraft. Yet, on the whole, the Hunter gave us
comparatively little trouble and her initial development was fairly
uneventful. We had sufficient time to get rid of a few bugs before the
annual display of the Society of British Aircraft Constructors at
Farnborough a few weeks later, in September; and I think that it was
fairly generally agreed that the Hunter, or the P1067 as it was still
known at that time, made a favourable impression at the 1951 show.

There were various estimates made of her speed, which was faster than any other British aircraft had flown at the show; and we certainly had the edge on the American F86, which had increased the world's speed record to 670.98 miles per hour.

Our general manager, Mr Spriggs, summed up the usefulness of the Hunter at that time when he said: "We believe that the P1067 will outfight any other known type of fighter interceptor flying today. The fact that the RAF ordered this new aircraft off the drawing board is the best testimony to its qualities."

We were certainly all very proud of our new aircraft and I had enormous satisfaction in its development flying. As I have already indicated it was a long slow process of finding out the necessary adjustments that had to be made before we could work it up to supersonic speeds—flight after flight, report after report, and always the design team working out modifications which would be incorporated in the aircraft by the patient Bill Turner, Bert Hayward and their flight shed team. Then came the day when Frank Bullen discovered that I had made a supersonic bang for the first time. Today you can take up the Hunter any time you like and put it through the sound barrier, knowing that it will perform perfectly.

The Hunter flew again at the SBAG at Farnborough in September 1952; and, since we had been working on it for a year and had penetrated the sonic barrier, it naturally travelled a good deal faster than it did during the previous September. Today, the Hunter is advertised as "the finest fighting aircraft in the world". It will not be very long before the Hunters coming off our production lines will re-equip the squadrons of Fighter Command.

It has been said that the aircraft industry bears some comparison to an iceberg, for while the public knows a good deal about its various productions, there are many more developments coming along under the surface.

While we were perfecting the Hunter, we were at the same time producing the next version of it—the Hunter F2, the prototype now being known as the Hunter F1. This later aircraft is powered with the Armstrong-Siddeley Sapphire instead of the Rolls-Royce Avon and differs in some other respects. The Sapphire has been type tested at 8,300 lbs thrust—higher than that of any other type tested jet engine in the world. The Hunter F2 looks very much the same as the Hunter F1, but with the extra power of the Sapphire engine it has higher performance.

The F2 was worked on throughout the summer, and there were speculations going on inside the firm as to whether it would fly before the end of November 1952. It arrived at Dunsfold during the middle of November, bearing the RAF roundels, not painted pale green like the F1 but finished in its aluminium service colour. On November 29th everything was set to take it up for the first time; directors arrived at Dunsfold and a number of people. But the weather clamped down and snow fell. Everybody had to go away disappointed.

The following day was a Sunday and during the early morning the clouds were still black and low. While I was at lunch the control tower rang me at home to report that the weather was clearing; and that there was a Seahawk available for me to have a look round to see what I thought about it.

This was more interesting than finishing my lunch! I had a short run round in the Seahawk and discovered a large area of gin clear sky. We agreed on a take-off time for round about 4 pm and various telephone calls were made to directors who might be able to get over to the airfield in time.

It was a darkish, nippy afternoon, the wind whipping the orange sock by the control tower; and Bert Hayward and his team all looked a bit white and peaked round the gills as they stood in raincoats and scarves when I climbed into the cockpit of the F2. Roy Chaplin and one or two other people were there; but unfortunately Sydney Camm was at a meeting of the committee of his golf club—he is a great golf enthusiast —and we were unable to get in touch with him. Compared with the first flight of the F1 there were very few people about—just as I preferred it. Gwen was there, too, she went up to see the take-off from the control tower, and I promised to be home in time for tea.

Dunsfold's black runway was glistening with rainwater and there were one or two thin pools about; the light was a bit gloomy but I was happy about everything and very keen to do this flight after the indecisions of the past few days. The F2 took off normally and the only slight hitch was that the nose wheel stayed down and would not retract. Bill Willis at the control tower told me about this very soon after I had taken off, and it confirmed the feeling I had already gained. I made various efforts to retract the wheel, and did a circuit, flying over the runway for Bill to let me know whether it was still down. It remained down, so there was nothing much more to be done. I landed after a quite satisfactory flight lasting twenty-two minutes. It was getting towards dusk and the flarepath had been lighted; I enjoyed my tea in front of the fire.

We are now doing developmental work on the F2, at Dunsfold and everything is proceeding normally; as the F2 is pretty well on the secret list still, there is not much I can say about it.

CHAPTER 14

# *Farnborough*

NOBODY interested in aeroplanes can go to the annual display of the Society of British Aircraft Constructors at Farnborough without experiencing a thrill of pleasure and, perhaps, of excitement. It is the shop window of Britain's aircraft industry; and every firm works for weeks beforehand to make sure that its wares are displayed to the best advantage both in the static and the flying displays. In the great tents and in the aircraft park are all the latest products—and millions of pounds worth of capital and machines are represented on that broad, grassy patch. The place is packed with people in the industry, with home and overseas buyers, politicians, and representatives of our three armed services as well as those from practically every country in the world.

It is a great occasion for the pilots who fly the aircraft entered by the many British firms. They have two jobs to do. The display lasts seven days, and the first four are devoted to showing off the performances of the aircraft to people whose business is flying, whether they are in the industry or in the services. The last three days are for the general public, and most people are interested more in an exhibition of flying and aerobatics rather than in technical performances.

So during the first four days, our job is to show to the industry and to the services such points as the ability of an aircraft to take off after a short run, the rate of climb or acceleration, the rate of roll, its manoeuvrability and how it handles at high or low speeds. On the final three days, our role amounts almost to a general flying display, using the aeroplane and its technical features to the utmost; and this is quite a popular pastime for us, especially as towards the end of the week we know the drill and can be fairly sure of our timing and positioning.

You have to train, or rehearse, for Farnborough in practically the same way as you do for any kind of show. Pilots must know their

160

machines thoroughly and their capabilities to the finest degree. There is little margin for errors when you are doing a fast run at 700 miles per hour or more at a height of about 50 feet, or aerobatics at low altitude; and you have to be absolutely certain of everything you are doing.

I learned a sharp lesson in the 1949 Farnborough show when I was demonstrating the Hawker N7/46, the prototype Seahawk. It had been my practice throughout the whole week to begin my display with an inverted fly-past from one end of the aerodrome to the other. I suppose that by Friday familiarity was breeding contempt, for in the roll-out from the inverted position to normal flight at about 100 feet I did not ease the stick far enough forward, and the nose of the aircraft fell.

I realized my error at once and ruddered hard, pulling the stick back as the aircraft rolled out, applying 10 G. Although my speed was about 450 miles an hour, a high speed stall occurred causing a noise like machine-gun fire.

Never have I seen the ground quite so near while flying upside down, nor have I had such a close view of one wing of a Balliol, with the biggest of roundels. Neither have I seen the pilots' tent from such close quarters while airborne, nor so many faces of startled pilots looking up.

The remainder of my demonstration was completed with thoughtful care. On landing, I walked to the pilots' tent. I found it hushed—and the bar open, early.

The moral is: never relax concentration or become careless.

The best preparation for Farnborough is to practise as much as possible at a safe height, until every manoeuvre can be carried out with not the slightest error. Everything is perfectly timed at these displays and you know exactly how long you will have for your performance, usually a total of five minutes from take-off to touch-down. It is particularly important to keep to the landing time, because the following aircraft may be coming in low and fast, and on time, and if you are late you will still be approaching with wheels and flaps down.

Five minutes is a meagre period for a high speed aircraft, which requires a wide sweep to turn and line up for its next manoeuvre; but a prolonged performance is boring for the spectators, and many aircraft have to fly during the display period.

It is, therefore, important to work out a precise programme; for instance, if you have an aircraft of sufficient performance, you begin by diving to reach sonic speed and cause a bang, so popular at the 1952 display. Then you work out a series of rolls, loops, or aerobatics in the looping plane, such as a half-loop and roll off, or a figure of eight. The manoeuvres should be varied in sequence to avoid repetition, and a few reversed turns interspersed.

Having mapped out your programme, you go through it at several thousand feet, first practising one manoeuvre at a time, and then joining them into a continuous series. In case there should be low cloud or bad weather during the display, it is advisable to find the minimum height required for such aerobatics as a loop, and the minimum speed at which it can be made.

One manoeuvre should lead into and leave the aircraft in a position to begin another, until the whole performance looks natural and easy. At the same time you work out an alternative programme to suit the weather if, for instance, the cloud base should become a little low or visibility deteriorate.

When you are satisfied with the routine at a safe height, you come lower and try it out, time after time, at low altitude over your own aerodrome, until you are happy about doing the first performance.

Constant practice is required to keep your hand in for demonstrations, which are part of a test pilot's job.

Besides the actual flying, there are a number of points you must bear in mind. You have to make sure that your various manoeuvres will be done before the centre of the crowd. You have to remember where the sun is so that you don't have people squinting into it while trying to watch you. You have to remember that wind can be a nuisance and cause a ragged performance; if you start manoeuvring across a strong wind you may drift and become badly placed and give an untidy show. We usually find that the best thing is to work out an imaginary line in front of the crowd—up and down a runway if that is possible—and then try to stick to it.

If you are doing a fast, low level run it is usually most effective to make a straight, long and low run-in parallel with the crowd and about 50 yards in front of it. You can give a display a bit more polish if you finish each manoeuvre clearly and cleanly by making a slight pause before beginning another; for instance, if you do a slow roll you could finish by holding the aircraft level for a second or two before going into a turn or perhaps some other aerobatic. In general a golden rule is: don't fly over the heads of the crowd. Quite apart from it being rather neck-breaking, it could also be dangerous. Another rule is: make sure the display can be seen by as many people as possible with, again if possible, the aircraft in their sight the whole time. This is rather easier said than done these days when you are flying at high speed and there are times when you cannot avoid disappearing temporarily from view. I feel that there is quite an art in show or display flying; and that it is great fun trying to perfect it.

I have taken part in four SBAC displays, all at Farnborough, from 1949 to 1952. In 1948 when I had just joined Hawker's, Wimpy Wade demonstrated the P1040 with great success, and Frank Murphy flew a Sea Fury. In 1949 I flew the prototype of the N7/46 and Wimpy the new swept-wing version of the N7, the P1052. There was rivalry between this machine and Mike Lithgow in the Supermarine 510, a swept-wing research development of the Attacker.

In 1950 I flew the N7/46 again, and Wimpy the P1081, a further development of the P1052. The Supermarine 535 made a spectacular appearance and again challenged the Hawker machine for the most impressive display. The 535 was more rugged in appearance and made more noise than the P1081 looking faster, perhaps, for this reason. In fact there was little to choose, but the rivalry for supremacy in performance produced some excellent displays from the two pilots, each a master of aerobatic and display flying.

The Venom arrived in 1950 and, with typical de Havilland showmanship, this machine and the night fighter version of the Vampire were prepared in time for the SBAC week. John Derry flew the Venom with magnificent skill, displaying his reverse roll for the first time. I remember particularly his spectacular roll off the top from take-off in a demonstration of this machine's climbing powers after a short take-off.

Few of us will ever forget John Cunningham showing the important new Comet for the first time, an aircraft which was to become the envy of the Americans and to open a new era in air transport. John has the happy knack of presenting a machine at its best angles and attitudes.

By far the most original manoeuvre of recent years at Farnborough was the Zura Cartwheel by the Polish test pilot Jan Zurakowski, flying for Gloster Aircraft in a Meteor 8 fully loaded with rockets. It consisted of a vertical climb at full throttle to some 4,000 feet where, at an appropriately low speed, one engine was fully throttled back; with the other engine at full throttle the Meteor performed a perfect cartwheel, nose over tail and tail over nose. The aircraft then began a spin, which Zura stopped at will, nicely lined up for starting the next manoeuvre.

Zura is one of the finest examples of test pilot-technician; he often calculates or reduces his own test results, sometimes causing the boffins a headache. He is now in Canada, test flying the CF 100 for Avro Canada, in which he recently exceeded Mach 1.

In 1951 I had to fly two aircraft at Farnborough, for Wimpy had been killed in the P1081 and there had been insufficient time to obtain another pilot, or for either Frank Murphy or Frank Bullen to convert to the P1052. I flew this aircraft, which had been adapted for naval flying and fitted with a hook; and also the P1067—the Hunter. This was the best SBAC display I can recall. We felt that Hawkers had it all their own way on this occasion; there was nothing to touch the P1067 for speed or, I think I may claim, grace of line.

One of the many interesting points about the 1952 Farnborough was that, for the first time, the sonic boom or bang was produced regularly for spectators.

Aircraft flying at, or near, the speed of sound cause "shock" waves of air pressure. They may be compared very roughly with the bow and stern waves of a ship moving quickly through water. Two waves are formed at speeds just below Mach I on the trailing edge of the wing—a small within a larger one. Another wave is also formed by the leading edge of the wing. These waves are present at and about sonic speed and roughly keep pace with the aircraft. They move ahead of the aircraft when it slows to subsonic speed.

When they reach the earth they cause up to three booms, or bangs, two of them fairly large, the third minor. Sometimes, after an aircraft has dived at supersonic speed, three white puffs may be seen in the sky. It seems that they usually form at the height of the cloud layer of the day, and it is suggested that they may be caused by a sharp fall in the pressure of the air, behind the waves which have just passed at sonic speed.

Supersonic bangs have been heard over varying areas on the ground. This is because aircraft have, so far, reached supersonic speed while diving towards the earth. The area over which the bangs are heard depends on the angle at which the aircraft is diving—the more acute the angle of the dive, the smaller is the area over which the bangs are heard, and vice versa.

It is believed that atmospheric conditions also contribute in causing the bangs to be heard over a smaller or wider area. This is the theory: the pressure wave—or pressure field—produced by the aircraft travels towards the earth in a horn-shaped path. Since the speed of sound increases with a rise in temperature, the pressure field will travel more quickly at lower altitudes, and the nearer it gets to the earth. This causes the horn pattern of the pressure waves to curve slightly upwards. For a start, after sonic speed has been reached and the aircraft has slowed down, the pressure field will travel along the same direction as the aircraft; as it nears the earth, it will curve up slightly and so overshoot the pilot's aiming point. It will also expand in area.

This tendency to curve is greatest in dives of shallow angles, with these results: if an aircraft diving at ten degrees generates a bang at 30,000 feet, the explosions will not reach the ground but will curve away upwards and eventually fade out. If it dives at thirty degrees, generating a bang at 30,000 feet, the bang will be heard over an area approximately six miles across and fourteen miles long. If it dives at forty-five degrees, generating a bang at the same height, the noise will be heard over an area approximately two-and-a-half miles across and four miles long.

As a very simple illustration, take a torch in a dark room. Imagine that it throws a light which curves slightly upwards. If you hold it at a reasonable height at a shallow angle, the light will not shine on the floor at all. But if you incline it gradually towards the floor, you will get a long, broadish pool of light; the sharper the angle of the torch, the smaller, and more concentrated, the pool of light will be. Roughly speaking the pool of light on the floor can be compared with the area of the ground over which the bangs are heard.

It has been noticed that some supersonic bangs seem louder than others. The present belief is that this is due to the height at which the aircraft is flying and the angle at which it is diving when it reaches sonic speed: noise increases in proportion to the lower altitude and sharper angle. It also seems that the area over which three bangs may be heard is sharply defined: observers only a few yards apart have reported hearing a different number of bangs and their assessment of the noise has also differed.

Although there has been some discussion of the bangs causing damage on the ground by blast effect, generally speaking the explosions caused by dives are harmless, though no doubt they are startling. On the other hand, it is possible that aircraft flying near one another at supersonic speed and within a range of about four miles may be affected. There have been reports of other aircraft being struck by a violent gust when explosions have been caused. Since it will not be long before sonic speed is reached in level flight, and not only by diving, investigation as to the effect on other aircraft flying in the same region seems most necessary.

Once aircraft can fly regularly at sonic speed in level flight, it is thought that explosions will not be heard on the ground unless they fly below 20,000 feet. But the effect of their speed may still be felt by another aircraft, and tests over a selected area would provide important information.

But we are straying rather far from Farnborough; as I have said, this is a simplified discussion of supersonic bangs, and theories about them are still being developed.

I have many memories of Farnborough; but those of 1952 will remain with me all my life. The death of John Derry and his observer, Tony Richards, together with the loss of twenty-eight spectators and the injury of many more was a great shock to everybody.

I was very fond of John Derry and admired him tremendously as a pilot. We had known each other for a long time, we met frequently and, of course, we had similar interests. His wife, Eve, and Gwen are great friends, too, and we have all spent many happy hours together. He had done more supersonic flying than any of us, and he was always so helpful in giving information gained from his own experiences.

I had watched him every day at Farnborough from the aircraft park and admired the way he could handle the de Havilland 110. After his performance was over, and he had landed, I had to be ready to take-off immediately, climb to about 40,000 feet and then come back and do my bit.

On that Saturday when John was killed, I had just arrived in the aircraft park in my car; and I had got out and was standing by it to watch him. He had been over to Hatfield to pick up the first prototype of the DH 110—he had been flying the second prototype during the earlier part of the week.

It was a lovely afternoon, and after he had made his supersonic bangs we could see a couple of puffs in the clear sky. John, with Tony, came on down and did their normal fly-past; and with this manoeuvre over, he began to slow down and turn back over the airfield, getting ready to go through his normal routine before landing.

The DH 110 blew to bits while it was in a moderate turn. Like everybody else, I was shocked to see the cockpit and the two engines flying through the air, landing some distance from me.

I imagine my first thoughts were like those of everybody else: poor old John and Tony. And Eve. And all those people who had been directly in the way of the engines and the cockpit. Then I began to wonder what could have caused the aircraft to split to pieces like that. One thing seemed fairly clear to me: it need not necessarily have had anything to do with supersonic flight.

There was nothing I could do. I stood discussing the accident with Les Colquhoun, of Supermarine, Bill Bedford, and Bert Hayward until it was time for me to get into the Hunter. I felt very sad at losing another good friend—so very many had gone during the war; later Hunk and Wimpy.

And now John Derry.

Soon I had to stop thinking about them. It was time for me to go off, but there was a bit of delay while the wreckage of the 110 was being cleared from the runway.

"Please keep to the right-hand side of the runway on take-off and mind the wreckage," I was told by control tower over the r/t.

"Roger," I replied—meaning that I understood and agreed.

"Are you going to climb and do a bang?" was the next question.

"That is roger."

"Will you soft-pedal your display over the crowd, please?"

"Roger."

I kept well clear of the wreckage on the runway and was soon pre-occupied climbing and going through my routine mentally. I always took off some ten minutes before my display was due to start to give myself time to reach about 40,000 feet and to get into the proper position for the dive on Farnborough.

It was a lovely day for flying. At 43,000 feet over Odiham I could see the airfield clearly. While sitting up there at that height I had more time to spare and to think in the lonely world above the scattered cloud, in the clear visibility under the darkening canopy of the stratosphere.

The cockpit was quiet and warm; everything was in first class order. It would be untrue to say that I was not disturbed and worried by John's death. I reflected that so little is known of supersonic flight; perhaps it could have had something to with the accident.

Then it was time to dive. The Hunter did its stuff perfectly, the bangs were heard by the crowd at the display, and with that visibility I should not have missed the mark.

When I landed I could see the ambulances still in the area where the DH had broken up. I hoped that many people had not been hurt. I thought about Gwen; and about Eve.

Gwen was not at the display that afternoon. She was in London and was shocked when she saw the posters of the evening papers saying that a test pilot had been killed at Farnborough, mentioning no name. She rang through to the control tower, and was told that I had finished my show and was just coming in to land.

Eve Derry had shown wonderful courage. I was deeply touched to learn later that day that though she, too, had seen John's aircraft break up, yet she had insisted on remaining to watch me go through my peformance. I felt that showed tremendous courage.

We spent a quiet and rather reflective evening and it was difficult to stop thinking of John and Eve, and Tony Richards and of all the people who had been killed and injured.

The next day the weather was indifferent. The Farnborough area was covered with cloud, which began at about 4,000 feet and went up to 23,000 feet. I could see no reason why I should not try to go through my usual routine for the final afternoon of the display, and cause some more sonic bangs.

There was one complication, and that was to make sure that the bangs would be heard by the crowd. As I knew I should not be able to see the airfield, it was necessary to get some mechanical help from the ground. This was provided, efficiently and enthusiastically, by the Farnborough ground control under Mr Bill Pendrey, who had successfully assisted during the week on several occasions.

The radar and radio fixing system at Farnborough combined with our Marconi homer at Dunsfold to direct me to the point where I should put the Hunter into its dive. And it was done in this way. I took off from Farnborough and climbed to 44,000 feet on instruments, flying in a south-westerly direction towards the Bournemouth area. From there, I was directed by the ground controller at Farnborough to turn east, pass south of the Isle of Wight, and then to fly along the English Channel. My position was being fixed at intervals of about one minute on the direction-finding angulator screen at Farnborough. I could see neither the land nor the sea, for cloud blotted everything out fairly soon after I had taken off. But the controller knew exactly where I was, and at the right moment he told me to turn north towards Dunsfold, so that I could have a steady run-in of at least fifteen miles.

As the Hunter approached Dunsfold, Hawker's controller took charge, and, passing rapid check vectors, directed me over Dunsfold on a northerly heading. When I was immediately over our airfield, Farnborough gave me an initial diving vector. I peeled off to port; a few seconds later I was given my final diving vector.

I could see nothing but a blanket of grey cloud below, and in a few moments the Hunter entered it, travelling at well over Mach 1. The bangs were caused, but they missed the airfield, and I was sorry to disappoint everybody. Either my angle of dive was too shallow, or I took up a position too close to Farnborough. We learned later that the bangs began at Camberley, a short distance away, and were heard all the way to Henley.

There is nothing really difficult about causing these bangs, once you know your aircraft and this drill for positioning it to the right spot. And to digress slightly, a similar form of control to that used during the display, was also used by the RAF Metropolitan sector of Fighter Command when Marshal Tito visited Duxford early this year. When I took up the Hunter, the cloud base was about 1,000 feet with complete eight-eighths coverage; the cloud tops were between 10,000 and 20,000 feet. Directed by the sector controller, I took up a position the required fifteen miles from Duxford at 43,000 feet, and was given a heading to dive on. It was accurate fixing, for a couple of healthy bangs were heard by the Marshal on the airfield; and later, when I had the honour of meeting him, he showed great interest in aircraft as well as sonic explosions.

I have much respect and some sympathy for the ground controller at displays and demonstrations where bangs are part of the programme. Everything must be run to time, and he has to get you to the right place almost at the right second, and even allow for the time that has to elapse as the explosion travels down to the ground.

But to get back to Farnborough. After I had dived the Farnborough D/F homed me back to the airfield where visibility was poor; but it was sufficiently good to let me go through a limited routine performance, with which I was now fairly familiar. I found it much harder to attend the private funeral of John Derry and Tony Richards. They were a great loss to aviation, and my deepest sympathy went out to Eve.

We know that test flying can be a risky business, but if you were never prepared to take a risk, you would never do anything. Travelling by train and by road is risky; and if you look at the statistics you will find that travelling by road is far more lethal than flying. Just consider the number of people killed on the roads in this country alone. If the same percentage number were killed by aircraft crashes every year I doubt whether many people would consider flying at all. But nobody dreams of not travelling by car, by bus, by motor-cycle or by bicycle.

We accept the risks of flying; and, for me, flying is just as great a thrill to-day as when I first went up in the old Avro 504K. One of the thrills of flying is to take up the Hunter to over 40,000 feet, up into the clear deep, sapphire blue. Down below, you can see the earth, far away—it is best to pick clear days for vertical dives in the Hunter. Now . . . at full-throttle you half-roll over and pull through. The nose of the Hunter is pointing straight down at the earth; and you are hanging forward in the straps, feeling as though you may slip out of them and fall forward at any moment. Now you are really beginning to move. The indicated speed begins to build up and so does the Mach number. Soon you are going straight down at the earth at supersonic speed. You can see the earth rushing up towards you. The needle on the altimeter is whirling madly round, reeling off thousands of feet as you go down, straight as an arrow. It's a wonderful thrill. When the Hunter is going down flat out you are falling at much more than 50,000 feet a minute.

Now the ground seems to be getting a little close. You ease back the throttle, and at something below 20,000 feet begin to start easing back the control column. The earth still seems to be rushing madly at you. But gradually the nose of the Hunter comes up above the horizon. You take a glance down; the earth is not far away but you are now flying parallel to it, straight and level. And now into a zoom?

Back with the control column, until the Hunter is pointing directly at the sky from which you have just ripped down. Now you are lying flat on your back in the cockpit. And this time it seems as though you are going to fall over backwards. Up, up you go, with the altimeter whirling again. You can easily shoot straight up for over 20,000 feet in the Hunter in a zoom from ground level, flying straight into space, into the blue, with very little sense of speed this time. Then you level off by pulling the Hunter on to its back and rolling out to level flight. Who would miss the thrill of flying?

In making a wide loop you use up a lot of sky, covering as much as 10,000 feet quite easily. In the Hunter the loop is not quite a circle; it is rather more oval. Up you go, over on your back, and then with a gentle movement of the control column round you come, round and down, and level out. Wonderful!

Doing a series of rolls is exhilarating, too. You can do as many as eight in the Hunter while passing over the length of an airfield. When you finish rolling, for a moment or two you feel that you are a bit "one-sided", as though you want to lean in the direction of the rolls you have just made. So, to even up your senses, you do a turn in the opposite direction.

For me there is no greater satisfaction than sitting in the cockpit of the Hunter, beautiful in design and construction, representing the thought and skill of so many people, and feeling it respond to the slightest movement of your fingers. It lives and is obedient to your slightest wish. You have the sky to play in—a great limitless expanse. But you have to be careful. Physically, you must be on the topline. You must be fit. You should not fly while you have a cold. Your senses must not be blurred in any way. Should you have a cold you can get excruciating pains in the head if you vary heights rapidly. And if your senses are blurred, your reflexes dull, the Hunter will still obey you—but you can both land up in trouble.

CHAPTER 15

# A Look Ahead

THERE will come a time, I suppose, when I shall have to give up experimental test flying and I must confess that I am not looking forward to it. But none of us is getting younger, and sooner or later in the normal course of time I shall become less physically fit, less able to stand the effects of testing aircraft at high speed; and my reflexes will gradually become slower.

One of the reasons why you must be fit to fly modern fighter aircraft is so that you may stand the effects of G—or gravity pull. To explain G as simply as possible: say you are sitting reading this book in an armchair. As you sit there, you are sitting at 1 G, that is your own weight.

Now imagine yourself in an aircraft. As you fly along, straight and level, you are sitting at 1 G, no matter at what speed the aircraft is travelling. Supposing the pilot sees an object sticking up straight ahead of him: he pulls back the control column, and up goes the aircraft, and up you go too. According to the steepness of the sudden climb your weight presses harder against the seat, and the weight of your body against the seat increases to, say, double its normal weight. You are now sitting there at 2 G. And so you can go on.

Supposing the pilot turns the aircraft sharply at speed. The weight of your body against the seat increases with the sharpness of its turn. Your weight may increase against the seat as the aircraft swings round to three, four, five and more times its weight. You are now sitting at 3 G, 4 G, 5 G—as the case may be. We call this acceleration.

So much for G. Now what about the effects of G?

As you sit in your chair reading at 1 G, your blood is circulating quite normally away from, and to, your head. What G does as it increases, is to cause the blood to drain away faster from your head—as G increases,

172

so does the blood flow away faster. And as the blood begins to drain away from your head and your brain, so your senses begin to be affected. First, you get a feeling or sense of blurred vision and greyness, and, as G increases, of darker greyness. Next, you lose your vision and black out. Eventually you would lose consciousness if you held too high a G for too long.

If you are fit it takes very little time to regain normal sight, and usually, normal sight returns as soon as acceleration is eased. But if you are not fit, if you have been to a party and still have a certain amount of alcohol in your blood—the old hangover—then it takes you longer to regain your normal faculties; you begin to lose sight and, maybe, consciousness much earlier and it takes you longer to regain your normal state again.

Normally you can stand four and a half G, or three and a half times your own weight, for a fairly sustained period without blacking out completely. The more you fly and pull G, the more your body becomes accustomed to withstanding acceleration—it is as though you go into training to stand up to G.

To help pilots withstand G a special suit can be worn, fitting tightly round the stomach and legs. This suit has an air valve which works automatically as G increases, and as the valve opens it inflates the suit. The suit, pressing harder and harder against your legs and stomach prevents the blood from draining into them and keeps more in the upper part of the body and head. The result of this pressure is that you can stand about 2 G more.

When in regular practice I can stand a sustained four and a half to five G and, should I wear a suit, about six and a half to seven G. You can go up to eleven or twelve G for a very short period without feeling the effects of blood draining from the head, but G of this order is not usually held for long as there is a danger of damaging the aircraft, which are not normally stressed to stand more. As a rule, I don't wear a G suit while testing. But in these days of high speed flying these suits are an absolute necessity for fighter pilots who may have to, and usually do, maintain high G for long periods during dog-fights. These manoeuvres are extremely tiring physically.

There is another kind of suit worn increasingly by pilots, and this is the pressure suit. It has to be put on if you are going to fly above 50,000 feet where the air is thin and its pressure so much less than at ground level. The pressure suit is skin tight and inflated with air; it maintains a constant pressure round the body at a great height. At the same time you wear a helmet with a glass face-piece and breathe pure oxygen. The general effect is to make you look a rather futuristic figure, or the popular idea of men from other planets.

These suits must be worn at great height whether the cabin is pressurized or not for, if the perspex hood of the cabin should crack— well, there you are, suddenly and very abruptly in thin, icy air and you would retain your consciousness for about eight to ten seconds. At the same time, in the low pressure at this height, your body might expand suddenly and cause physical damage.

Normally the pressure in a cabin of an aircraft flying at 50,000 feet is much the same as the actual pressure at 25,000 feet. I have had a canopy crack while flying at 40,000 feet, and it felt as though I had been hit sharply on the chest. I was very glad to be wearing a pressure waistcoat.

I suppose that you could say that G suits and pressure suits are part and parcel of the business of flying faster and higher. Some people are inclined to ask: where is this urge to fly faster and higher taking us; what good does it do? Maybe it is just human nature; if man had not been curious and wanted to improve things, perhaps he would still be living in a cave and going out to catch his Sunday dinner with a stone axe.

It seems inevitable that there will always be competition for higher speeds, if not for defence then for the sake of the development of aircraft and engines. We at Hawker's are now looking ahead to the time when we may have a fighter that will fly at Mach 2, or about 1,300 miles per hour.

I have often discussed this subject with Vivian Stanbury and he tells me that we may expect to reach this speed in level flight by about 1960. There will be problems to be solved in providing both the power and aircraft design before this speed can be achieved. To take some of the problems of power first, we know that a jet engine can become more powerful and develop more thrust with what is known as re-heat.

Not to be too technical, re-heat can be explained this way: the ordinary jet engine swallows a quantity of air; about one-quarter of that air entering a jet is used in being burnt with fuel, the remaining three-quarters being heated to a moderate extent but passing out of the engine unburnt. Re-heat takes that unused three-quarters and uses it all up with the burning of additional fuel. The faster a jet aircraft flies, the more

36.,

Hawker Sea Hawk—half roll and down!

37.,

With Winston Churchill, who was Honorary Commodore of 615
RAuxAF Squadron, at the time I commanded the Squadron—Biggin
Hill, 1951.

38.,

Our Hawker Tomtit G-AFTA, at Biggin Hill, 1954.

39.,

Hawker test pilots; (top to bottom) Hugh Merewether, Frank Bullen, Frank Murphy, Neville Duke and Bill Bedford.

40.

Celebrations in 1976—the twenty-fifth anniversary of the successful Hunter.

efficient its engines become. And it is known that with re-heat the thrust of jets flying at Mach 2 will be more than doubled.

You can imagine that the high temperatures generated in a jet engine, with re-heat being used all the time, is going to be pretty fierce. And here we run into perhaps the biggest problem of all: to find metals that will be capable of withstanding that heat without losing their strength or changing their shape. It is impossible to cool the engine, so you would have to insulate the aircraft structure. And insulation is another problem.

The search at the moment is for light, strong metals that will stand up to heat. Duralumin is being used but it loses some of its strength at high temperatures. Another metal that is strong, light and heat-resisting, is titanium, but at the moment its stage of development is about the same as that of duralumin some forty years ago. It is not yet a commercial proposition.

In addition to heat from the engine, heat from the flow of air against the aircraft and particularly the cabin at great speed is also a problem. You will remember that this had to be taken into account by the High Speed Flight at Tangmere. It may be, however, that this particular problem may not be very difficult to overcome, for already work on glass fibre laminate seems to indicate that an answer may be found. This fibre laminate is light, strong, heat-resistant, and fairly easy to mould. It can be given a tensile strength of up to 50,000 lbs a square inch, which is pretty strong.

Now we come to the problem of design. This is chiefly to do with the aircraft's wings—to get thinner and sharper-edged wings that remain strong and firm and help the aircraft to cut through the air more easily.

The faster a machine flies, the more it disturbs the air as it pushes its way through. With a thick or blunt wing at speed the air is bumped— you might say—at a sharpish angle upwards and downwards on either side of the wing. This angle is reduced as the wing is made thinner. As a rough example, supposing you take a kitchen knife and get somebody to hold a piece of paper with two hands so that the edge is facing you. If you cut the paper from the edge inwards with the knife, which will not be very sharp, you will work your way through the paper with a bumpy motion. But if you cut with a razor blade you will slice through quite easily.

One of the reasons why the delta wing has been introduced is to get this sharp-edged characteristic, together with greater depth, and so increase the strength and carrying capacity of a wing. The length of a wing—the distance between the leading or front edge and the trailing or rear edge—is known technically as the chord. And the chord of a delta wing is long, since the wing stretches from just behind the nose of the aircraft to the tail; and therefore it may be made thinner in relation to its length. Since drag is related to thickness-chord ratio, a delta wing can have low drag although having depth for storage. At the same time, the delta shape maintains the sweep-back of a wing which has been found necessary for flying at high speeds.

The swept-back wing has its advantages for flying at speed; but it also has its disadvantages when an aircraft is flying at low speed. There has been a tendency for some aircraft with swept-back wings to drop a wing if the machine is flown too slowly. But this can be avoided by careful and special design. One remedy is to fit slats, providing small auxiliary airfoils at the wing-tips on the leading edges. Another is the crescent wing.

With crescent wings you have the sweep back, necessary for high speed; but you also have their tips of the wings levelling out again, almost straight. The advantage of crescent wings is that they enable an aircraft to have the correct wing sweep and thickness for high speed; and they also have a straight wing-tip which can prevent a wing dropping at low speed.

The span of the wing is also important—that is the length of the wing from its root to its tip: the longer the span in relation to chord, the more is the lift that will be developed.This is particularly important for high altitude flight where the air is thin.

What we are now seeing with the development of various wings is an endeavour to provide an aircraft with thin, strong, swept wings. Some people think the delta is the answer, others believe in the crescent; others again feel that the straight wing may return for supersonic flying.

Now you may say: if fighter aircraft can be built to fly at 1,300 miles an hour then so can bombers and, from a defence point of view, one will cancel the other.

An interesting point here is that while we hope to produce a fighter to fly at 1,300 miles an hour comparatively soon, it may be a long time before bombers reach this speed for the cost of building and flying bombers at supersonic speeds would be colossal.

Once you reach Mach .95 the increase in drag is immense. When you begin to come up against the sonic barrier the drag is increased by three to four times, and the increase in fuel consumption to meet the need for more power is roughly the same figure. And the cost of a fleet of bombers, in terms of fuel consumption and loss of payload, pushing through the sonic barrier—let alone the cost of building them—would be enormous. For the same reason of expense, many people think that it will be a long time before civilian services attempt to fly at more than about Mach .95. The cost of supersonic flying would be prohibitive for commercial purposes. There is a possibility, however, that some new form of fuel—perhaps atomic—may be an answer for both civil and military aircraft.

It seems that, for the moment, the further development of the bomber will be in the field of the guided missile—the V2 of the last war. The trend seems to be for their increasing development and use. This in turn poses the question of defence.

It may be that one method of defence against the guided missile will be the rocket-powered interceptor fighter, or guided defensive missile. Something on these lines might occur: the moment a guided missile is released in enemy territory its path is mapped by radar, and a defensive missile shot off to intercept it at a selected point. The rocket motor carries its own oxygen and is not limited to any height like a jet engine.

It may be looking rather far ahead to suggest the use of rocket interceptors in this way, particularly as a rocket motor is most expensive, burning enormous quantities of oxygen and fuel—something like fifteen times the weight of fuel used by a jet for the same running time. But rocket fighters could be used for intercepting bombers at very high altitude.

In time, another development of the guided missile may have civilian uses. In the very distant future we may have things something like the V2, fitted with rudimentary wings, carrying passengers; they may work up great power for initial acceleration for a few minutes to great altitude and then glide or coast the rest of the distance—in very much the same way as an electric train cuts off its motor and coasts for a portion of the distance between stations.

Such a method of gliding could be fairly economical for great distances. All the available power would be used in that quick, short acceleration; and less fuel would be burnt for that burst than if you burnt the fuel at a slower rate over the whole distance. Suppose, for argument's sake, it requires 1,000 gallons of fuel to reach the required altitude. If you double the thrust you will reach that height using less fuel, for it is a fact that you would go up in less than half the time.

All this is getting pretty well into the future; and we still have a number of present problems on our hands in working up aircraft to fly at higher speeds. One of them is what is known as "flutter" of aerofoils or control surfaces.

Without being technical the problem may be explained this way: a flag flutters or quivers in a strong breeze, for its cloth is very flexible. It would not flutter if it were stiff, like a weather-cock for example. Now from the point of view of an aircraft, if its wings and tail surfaces are not sufficiently stiff they will flutter at very high speeds, possibly with disastrous results. The problem is to provide the wings and tail surfaces with the necessary stiffness without increasing their weight too much.

Another problem is to avoid buffeting. This is caused by airflow at high Mach number breaking down on a part of the aircraft and forming shock waves, causing the machine to shake.

There are also a number of problems that have to do with the comfort and the safety of the pilot. They include the provision of heating at high altitude; keeping the pilot cool while he is flying at high speed; protecting him from the noise caused by the rush of air over the cabin and through such things as ventilating holes; and also making sure that the ejector seat will work efficiently while the aircraft is travelling at high speed, allowing him to bale out quickly.

Helping to solve these problems and to develop new types of aircraft are all part of the experimental test pilot's job. Nowadays, perhaps, it is not easy to become a test pilot. It is only by flying with one of the services, that a pilot can obtain the necessary flying experience to consider such an occupation. It is also necessary to attend the Empire Test Pilots' School if the training is to be complete. With this experience, and having spent a period testing at a service establishment, such as the Aeroplane and Armament Experimental Establishment at Boscombe Down or the Royal Aircraft Establishment at Farnborough, the prospective test pilot is equipped for employment by the leading aircraft firms as a pilot on experimental work.

A test pilot has to be very fit. He has to get used to wearing all sorts of equipment—pressure suits, G suits, pressure waistcoats and masks, to withstand very high G and high rates of climb and descent perhaps in the order of 60,000 feet per minute, and flying at heights up to 40,000 feet without a pressure cabin. High flying in particular calls for complete fitness and freedom from the unpleasant affliction of "bends" or lack of oxygen in the blood stream which causes extreme pain. Deep sea divers can experience a similar effect.

A test pilot, particularly a pilot engaged on experimental or research flying, must thoroughly enjoy doing his work and love flying for its own sake. If the day should come when he does not enjoy flying or if he loses interest in the work, then it is time to seek another occupation. It is true, I think, that the more flying you do, within reason, the more you want to fly. I found this so on operations during the war and still find it so today.

There is normally no guarantee of employment for a test pilot after he retires and his whole career and livelihood depend on his remaining fit and keen.

These facts are known to all test pilots but it is significant that there has never been a lack of men to come forward and take up a test flying career. The number of pilots required is limited and the qualifications severe.

Anybody embarking upon such a career should realize all these points, but I think they will find the work sufficient reward in itself and achieve a tremendous sense of satisfaction and pride in taking part in a job which, I feel, has no equal in any other walk of life in its opportunities for initiative, skill and technical achievement.

# Addendum

IN the summer of 1953, the Hunter was well into the development stages for the RAF and at Hawkers we had a very fast Hunter, the original prototype fitted with re-heat. During the course of the flight development programme it was decided to make an attempt on the World Air Speed Record. The Americans had only recently achieved 715.75 miles per hour (1,151.64 kilometres per hour), when Lieutenant Colonel William F Barnes secured it for his country, flying an F 86D Sabre.

Flying from RAF Tangmere, the all-red Hunter (WB188) achieved 727.63 miles per hour (1,170.76 kilometres per hour) off Littlehampton on September 7th. This was to be the last attempt made in the United Kingdom using the original FAI regulations requiring the record to be the best of four three-kilometre runs below 100 metres (328 feet). Flying as low as possible the sensation of speed was exhilarating but left little margin for error.

It was during a previous attempt on September 1st that we nearly came unstuck when one undercarriage leg was sucked out with a big bang as I ran in over Bognor Pier, passing about 300 feet with speed building to 700 miles per hour! The Hunter whipped over the vertical and I was nearly into the sea. Such was the strength of the Hunter that it held together *in extremis*. I landed her back at Dunsfold on two wheels without too much further damage. The Hawker Experimental Department had the wing off, repaired at Kingston in double quick time and we were back in the air on the seventh to make the record run that same day.

This was all nicely timed to attend the Farnborough Air Show on the following day and the day after that it was into the Rapide and lunch with the Prime Minister at Chequers! Flying from Dunsfold on the nineteenth we gained the 100 kilometre closed circuit speed record of

180

709.2 miles per hour. This lovely aeroplane now resides in the good hands of the RAF Cosford Museum.

I last flew a Hunter in 1983 to commemorate the thirtieth anniversary of these World Speed Records and to raise some funds for the Stoke Mandeville Hospital. The flight over Tangmere and along the old High Speed flight course off Littlehampton stirred a few memories. It is a source of quiet satisfaction that the Hunter turned out to be such a great success and became a classic fighter loved and acclaimed by pilots. Some two thousand were produced and served with no less than eighteen air forces around the world.

Forty-three years after it first flew, the Hunter was still in front line service with the Swiss Air Force in large numbers but sadly not now. Neither is it now in service in this country with any RAF establishments but many are still in private hands throughout the world, and most particularly in the United Kingdom, Europe, the United States, New Zealand, Australia and South Africa. The Chilean Air Force still possess some but they are not now in regular use if at all. What a wonderful service record it enjoyed though, and with justification!

Throughout 1954 and into the summer of 1955, the Hunter test programme continued. By this time the Hunter was in RAF service, 43 Squadron having received the first ones at the end of July 1954, but service and company testing is an on-going ritual. In August 1955 I was carrying out gun-firing tests at sea level off Littlehampton at 700 miles per hour when there was a sudden bang which shook the Hunter. I throttled back immediately, scanning the instruments, but I could neither see nor feel any damage. However, as soon as I began to open up again, the engine was decidedly rough—temperature well off the clock—and then it stopped.

I managed to glide the aeroplane back towards Ford, trying to save the aeroplane. There is little use in a test pilot, having once discovered a problem, deciding to leave it and bale out. Either he or someone else will only run into it again if the reason is not discovered and corrected. There is, of course, a fine dividing line between loss of aeroplane and pilot and just the loss of an aeroplane, but that is all part of the test pilot's judgement. As some might put it—that's what one is paid for!

I got the machine down, thinking to myself that it was a turbine blade failure due to an engine surge whilst firing the four 30mm Aden guns and so it proved. However, for getting the Hunter safely back on the deck, I was surprised but honoured to receive the Queen's Commendation for Valuable Service in the Air.

Two days later, after an engine change, I went back down to Ford to collect the aeroplane. Everything seemed in order and take-off was no problem. As I cleared 1,000 feet, with Chichester Harbour just below me, I found that the throttle control only gave me idling thrust. I was suddenly faced with very few options.

RAF Thorney Island, which was almost underneath me, was the nearest aerodrome so I dropped down towards it. Due to my position I arrived with too much airspeed for a normal landing but insufficient excess speed to make a circuit in order to land on the main runway. Losing height I tried to put it down across the airfield on a rough grass surface, the ASI showing about 200 miles per hour. Touching down on this uneven surface put the poor old Hunter into a series of bounces that comes with a tricycle undercarriage which puts the machine's centre of gravity well aft. Something had to be done quickly as I was fast running out of landing space and in any event the Hunter was virtually out of control. I selected "wheels-up" but only one wheel retracted although it was enough to avert a fatal stall off the top of one of the rapidly increasing bounces.

Sitting helplessly in the cockpit, I jettisoned the hood and cut the fuel while the aeroplane careered into a number of arcs, I had no control over my destiny whilst being shaken unmercifully. Reaching the edge of the aerodrome it hurtled across a ditch before crunching nose first into a sea-wall on the other side. The machine broke up but I emerged from the mess with only cuts and bruises but aching badly. I can't remember how much pain I had at that precise moment, but it was later found that I had in fact fractured my spine. The problem with the Hunter had been caused by a small particle of fluff in a fuel control valve.

I was on my back and in a plaster-cast for a while but was able to return to flying, although still in plaster. I suffered a good deal of discomfort in my back at times but recovered reasonably well and I was able to continue the Hunter development. This included gun-firing trials to clear up some problems we were still having.

All went well, that is until May 9th 1956, when the crunch came in the literal sense—I crushed a disc and damaged my back following a very heavy landing in the P1099. The vertical impact was sufficient to also dislodge some teeth fillings!

The reason for this little adventure was that Hawkers had the P1121 private venture air superiority strike aircraft under construction at Kingston. In the mock-up layout the view from the cockpit appeared marginal, particularly in the landing attitude and it was decided to simulate the windscreen arrangement on the development Mark 6 Hunter—P1099. I think we proved the point! The project was eventually abandoned at Hawkers who then turned their attention to vertical take-off development.

I was now in big trouble and out of action flat on my back for a long time and in extreme pain. I eventually took to the air again after five months of useless inaction but after a few flights in October 1956, I realised that I could not take more than very limited "G" forces without considerable discomfort. The Hawker Company had been extremely tolerant and could not have been more helpful and understanding with the problem but I felt I could not remain on as a "lame duck" chief test pilot. It was mutually agreed and now quite obvious that I could not do the job any further and I sadly resigned.

I was very sad indeed to leave Hawkers where I had spent many happy years. It was a wonderful firm to work for and I feel honoured and privileged to have had that good fortune.

At least I left the company with a brilliant team of test pilots. Bill Bedford, who had been carrying the load of Hawker development during my indisposition, took over as Chief Test Pilot. He and Hugh Merewether subsequently did a magnificent job in the development of vertical take-off with the P1127—later to become the successful Harrier. Hugh, in turn, became Chief Test Pilot being followed in this capacity by Duncan Simpson. Frank Murphy, Frank Bullen, David Lockspeiser and Don Lucey maintained there meticulous standards they always set in flight testing the production Hunters.

*       *       *

For the next couple of years I cast around for another way of life but flying was really the only thing I wanted to do. I filled in this period in the wilderness with various part-time flying jobs and eventually decided to get a commercial pilots licence and fly for a living—as opposed to test flying!

During these wilderness years of 1957–58 I managed to keep my hand in on freelance flying and consultancy work with Fairey Aviation and Field Aircraft Services, amongst others. The flying was varied but limited and included an element of testing with Field Aircraft Services, on a variety of types, including F 86 and CF 100 Sabres for the Royal Canadian Air Force. I flew anything I could get my hands on, from a splendid Tiger Moth delivery from Croydon to Dublin, to a fifty-hour flight with a piston engine Provost to Rangoon for the Burmese Air Force. Much of 1958 and 1959 was taken up with flight testing the Garland-Bianchi "Linnet" light two-seater.

We had formed a bit of a trio at Field Aircraft and impecably led by Ken Burvill, we managed another Provost delivery to Khartoum for the Sudanese Air Force but lost one on the way when Andrew "Pants" Bloomer ditched some miles off Tarquinia on the Nice–Rome leg. Being a former Navy pilot he elected to put down on the sea rather than bale out—although the options were discussed over the r/t at some length whilst he was on the glide down. I thought we had lost him that time; although he put it down with great expertise there was a bit of a sea running and the aircraft immediately went on its back when the fixed undercarriage touched the water. It seemed an age before he literally bobbed to the surface. By buzzing the harbour at Tarquinia I was eventually relieved to see a fishing boat put out and follow me to the rescue. A well-oiled Andrew was eventually located in a harbour wine bar very late that night. The splendid Italians had been extremely hospitable and I think they enjoyed the adventure.

Andrew was a great character and fun to fly with—never a dull moment with him around but he had been lucky on this occasion, it being a very cold February day and a very cold sea. The sequel to this was a replacement delivery in April 1959 taking Gwen along as an auto-pilot and a return flight with a load of monkeys in a DC6 of the Africargo Service.

In the winter of 1959-60 I grappled with a correspondence course for a full commercial pilots licence and civil instrument rating in order to take up a part-time appointment with Sir George Dowty, as his personal pilot. The Dowty Group, founded by Sir George before the war, was and is, a major supplier of components for air forces and aviation worldwide.

This job introduced me to quite another aviation experience flying all over Europe in a DH Dove in all weathers, day and night, to all sorts of interesting places while meeting all sorts of interesting people. This included the Messerschmitt design team at Munich, and Heinkel and Dornier on lovely Lake Constance.

I formed Duke Aviation Limited for the purpose of operating on charter and executive work with the Dove and my own Piper Comanche which had previously been operated by Donald Campbell. This also enabled me to carry out some contract freelance test flying for a number of companies.

As time went by the executive use of the Dove by the Dowty Group had expanded to a full-time requirement and so in 1969 I handed over operations to McAlpine Aviation, so that I could expand my test flying commitments, in particular with Miles Aviation as their nominated test pilot.

Sadly the following year, there was an accident with the Dowty Dove at Wolverhampton and both pilots were killed. I was asked to revive Dowty Group flying with another Dove and eventually set up the operation with a full-time two-man crew. The Dove was followed over the years by King Air 100 and 200 aircraft. I relinquished this responsibility to the very capable hands of Captain Don Ward and Captain Tony Watts in 1979.

*    *    *

While with the Dowty-Rotol Group, I tested their ducted fan developments and later, with Edgley Aircraft Limited, flew the "Optica" certification and development tests from 1984-86. The following year it was with Brooklands Aerospace Group as company test pilot. Then more Optica work and also work on the Fieldmaster (crop dusting) aeroplane and its development into the Firemaster for water bombing. I was test flying until 1994 at the age of seventy-four and have been a private owner of a Piper Warrior since 1995.

The old back problem has never gone away and there remain constant encounters with occasional immobility but fortunately I have retained my medical flying category. I have flown some two hundred and thirty different aeroplane types, all of which has helped fill a good many flying log books and taken me to many parts of the world.

Sailing is my diversion and (some of the time) my wife Gwen enjoys this part of our lives together. Over the last forty-nine years we have sailed in North European and Mediterranean waters. All my recent boats I have named "High Flight" and here's why:

Oh, I have slipped the surly bonds of Earth
And danced the skies on laughter-silvered wings;
Sunward I've climbed and joined the tumbling mirth
Of sun-split clouds—and done a hundred things
You have not dreamed of—wheeled and soared and swung
High in the sunlit silence: hovering there,
I've chased the shouting wind along, and flung
My eager craft through footless halls of air.

Up, up the long, delerious burning blue
I've topped the wind-swept heights with easy grace
Where never lark, or even eagle ever flew—
And, while the silent lifting mind I've trod
The high untrespassed sanctity of space,
Put out my hand and touched the face of God.

*(Written by Pilot Officer John Gillespie Magee Jr,
killed in action with No 412 Squadron RCAF in 1941.)*

The war from Biggin Hill, the Western Desert, Tunisia and over Italy sometimes seem so very far away, but at other times so near and so very clear. Yet in over sixty years of flying, those three years are merely a fraction of the time I've spent in the sky. In a way, test flying has always been to me a mental continuation of operational flying—in fact our losses in the five year post-war period amounted to thirty-two of our test pilots. A peacetime attrition rate unsustainable even under wartime operational flying.

Test flying, like wartime flying, has its moments of danger, of apprehension, when one's skill, knowledge and experience are one's only ally. But both have given me enjoyment as well as sadness. The loss of a friend in action is no less sorrowful than the loss of a test pilot friend such as John Derry, or Mike Lithgow.

Now, over eighty years old, some people think it might be time to give up flying but when I get airborne the old adrenalin flows and the same interest and dedication seems to be there. It's too late to stop anyway. Perhaps when it ceases to be fun.

One doesn't make all the right decisions in life, but I got two right. The first was to make flying my career and the second was to marry Gwen. And one thing is for certain; I would not have missed either for the world—especially the latter!

Life is all luck and I have had more than my fair share of the commodity but what fate decreed that I should be blessed with the greatest luck of all in the shape of Gwen? We are not just very happily married, we are very, very good friends.

Neville Duke,
Hampshire,
January 2003

# Record of Service

RAF Depot, Uxbridge.
RAF Padgate, Liverpool.
No. 4 ITW Bexhill and Devon.
No. 13 EFTS RAF White Waltham—first Solo 6th Sept 1940.
No. 1 EFTS Hatfield.
No. 5 FTS Sealand.
No. 5 FTS Tern Hill—"Wings" Feb 1941.
No. 58 OTU Grangemouth.
No. 92 Squadron, RAF Biggin Hill—April 1941.
Posted to Middle East November 1941.
No. 112 Squadron, Western Desert, November 1941.
   Shot down by Obfw Otto Schulz of JG27, November 30th 1941.
   Shot down by pilot of JG27, December 5th 1941.
   Awarded DFC, March 1942.
   Completed first tour April 1942 having flown one hundred and sixty-one operational sorties in two hundred and twenty-one operational hours; Fighter School, Suez, April 1942.
No. 92 Squadron, 18th November 1942—Flight Lieutenant January 1943.
Awarded bar to DFC January 1943.
Awarded DSO March 1943.
Completed second tour April 1943 having flown one hundred and thirty-two further sorties in two hundred and three operational hours.
No. 73 OTU Abu Sueir, as CFI—Squadron Leader.
No. 145 Squadron, March 1944, Italy—Commanding Officer.
   Awarded second bar to DFC, May 1944.
   Brought down by flak June 7th 1944.
   Completed third tour September 20th 1944 after one hundred and

188

ninety-three operations in two hundred and eighty-eight operational hours. Total operational sorties four hundred and eighty-six during seven hundred and twelve operational flying hours.
Returned to United Kingdom, October 1944.
Test Pilot attached to Hawkers, January 1st 1945.
No. 4 ETPS Course, Cranfield, January 1946.
Awarded Czech War Cross 1946.
High Speed Flight, June 1946.
Aircraft and Armament Experimental Establishment, Boscombe Down, March 1947.
Awarded AFC, 1948.
Resigned Commission June 1948 to join Hawkers as Test Pilot.
Appointed Chief Test Pilot 1951.
Squadron Leader in Royal Auxiliary Air Force, commanding 615 Squadron 1950-51.
Awarded OBE January 1953.
Awarded Queen's Commendation for Valuable Service in the Air, 1955.
Relinquished Hawker appointment late 1956 due to fractured back and spinal injuries sustained in Hunter crash following engine failure.
Freelance flying and consultancy work, 1957-60.
Personal Pilot to Sir George Dowty, of the Dowty Group, 1960-69, and 1970-79.
Formed Duke Aviation Limited, 1960-1982.
Brooklands Aerospace Group 1987.
Company and Freelance Test Pilot.
Optica flight test and development.
Fieldmaster and Firemaster aircraft testing.

## Combat Successes 1941-44

| Squadron/Date | Destroyed | Probable | Damaged | Aircraft | Remarks |
|---|---|---|---|---|---|
| **1941** | | | | | |
| 92 Squadron | | | | Spitfire V | |
| 26 April | | | Me 109F | "Y" R6904 | Channel |
| 23 June | Me 109F | | Me 109F | "Y" R6904 | Circus No. 20, Le Touquet |
| 25 June | Me 109F | | | "Y" R6904 | Circus No. 23, St Omer |
| 9 August | | | Me 109F | "X" W3319 | Sweep, St Omer, |
| 31 August | | | | — | Convoy patrol |
| | | | | | |
| 112 Squadron | | | | Tomahawk | |
| 21 November | CR42 | | | "F" AK402 | Tobruk, shared with PO Butch Jeffries and Sgt Carson |
| 22 November | Me 109F | | | "F" AK402 | Ofhr Waskott of I/JG27 baled out—PoW |
| 30 November | Fiat G50 | | Me 109F | "F" AK402 | El Gobi area |
| 4 December | Macchi 200 | Ju 87 | | "F" AN337 | Tobruk airfield |
| 22 December | | Ju 52 | | "L" AK354 | Megrun airfield shared with Sgt Carson |
| | | Ju 87 | | "L" AK354 | |
| **1942** | | | | Kittyhawk | |
| 14 February | Macchi 200 | | | "V" AK578 | South West of Acrona |
| 14 February | Macchi 200 | | | "V" AK578 | With Sgt Reid of 3 RAAF Sqn |
| **1943** | | | | | |
| 92 Squadron | | | | Spitfire Vb/c | |

| Date | | | | Details |
|---|---|---|---|---|
| 8 January | Macchi 202 | | "R" ER220 | S Ten Tellerchi of 18 Gruppo—baled out—PoW |
| 11 January | Macchi 202 | | "S" ER336 | Magg Gustavo Garretto of 18 Gruppo—baled out—PoW |
| 11 January | Macchi 202 | | "S" ER336 | |
| 21 January | Ju 87 | | "R" ER220 | Pilot baled out, III/StG3 |
| 1 March | Macchi 202 | | "R" ER281 | North West of Medenin, both baled out—one was |
| 1 March | Macchi 202 | | "R" ER281 | S Ten Antonio Roglai, of 3 Stormo; PoW |
| 3 March | Me 109F | | "R" ER281 | North East of Gabes—III/JG77 pilot |
| 4 March | Me 109F | | "R" ER281 | Uffz Herbert Muller, I/SG2 |
| 4 March | Me 109F | | "R" ER281 | Baled out—PoW |
| 7 March | Me 109F | | "R" ER281 | Baled out—PoW |
| 7 March | Me 109F | | "R" ER281 | Ltn Heinz Schieder, I/SG2 |
| 25 March | Me 109G | Ju 88 | ER689 | |
| 29 March | Me 109G | | "R" ER121 | Gabes area |
| | | | Spitfire IX | |
| 16 April | SM82 | | EN333 | Cap Bon |
| 16 April | SM82 | | EN333 | Cap Bon |
| **1944** | | | | |
| **145 Squadron** | | Me 109G | Spitfire VIII | |
| 13 May | Me 109G | | "J" JG241 | Perugia area |
| 14 May | Me 109G | | "J" JG241 | Cassino area |
| 21 May | FW 190 | | "J" JG241 | North East of Velletri |
| 21 May | FW 190D (long nose) | | "J" JG241 | North East of Velletri |
| 7 September | Me 109G | | "J" MT775 | Near Rimini |
| 7 September | Me 109G | | "J" MT775 | Near Rimini |

# Index

192